LEADER-MANAGERS
in the
PUBLIC SECTOR

WITHDRAWN

LEADER-MANAGERS
in the
PUBLIC SECTOR
Managing for Results

MICHAEL S. DUKAKIS and JOHN PORTZ

M.E.Sharpe
Armonk, New York
London, England

Library of Congress Cataloging-in-Publication Data

Dukakis, Michael S. (Michael Stanley), 1933–
  Leader-managers in the public sector : managing for results / by Michael S. Dukakis and John
Portz.
    p. cm.
  Includes bibliographical references and index.
  ISBN 978-0-7656-2141-2 (hardcover : alk. paper)—ISBN 978-0-7656-2142-9 (pbk. : alk. paper)
  1. Leadership—United States. 2. Government executives—United States. 3. Organizational
effectiveness—United States. I. Portz, John, 1953– II. Title.

  JK421.D85 2010
  352.23´60973—dc22   2010018816

Printed in the United States of America

The paper used in this publication meets the minimum requirements of
American National Standard for Information Sciences
Permanence of Paper for Printed Library Materials,
ANSI Z 39.48-1984.

∞

| IBT (c) | 10 | 9 | 8 | 7 | 6 | 5 | 4 | 3 | 2 | 1 |
| CW (p) | 10 | 9 | 8 | 7 | 6 | 5 | 4 | 3 | 2 | 1 |

Contents

Preface

These opening pages are an opportunity to share with our readers a brief glimpse into why we decided to write this book as well as to acknowledge those, and especially our leader-managers, who were willing to take time out of busy schedules to make it all possible.

We share a belief in and a commitment to the value and importance of public service. Although our career paths were markedly different in getting here, both of us teach public policy and public management to undergraduate and graduate students in a way that we hope will help our students develop the skills they need to be effective public servants. In fact, we are missionaries for public service, and we make no bones about it.

Michael S. Dukakis served as chief executive of the Commonwealth of Massachusetts for a dozen years and stood on the national stage as a presidential candidate. John Portz has been a college professor for most of his adult career, but he has not stayed in the ivory tower. He has managed programs at the university level, has focused much of his work on state and national educational policy, and has served and continues to serve in elective local office.

For those reasons, we understand the challenges that leader-managers in the public sector face and the critical importance of developing the skills they need to be able to get things done in the often turbulent and complicated world of American politics. We work in a political science department that is focused on preparing young people for careers in public service.

We have been colleagues for nearly twenty years, and our conversations in the hallway would often focus on issues of leadership and management. How could we better prepare our students—who included twenty-year-old under-graduates as well as seasoned professionals in our mid-career programs—to meet the challenges of working and achieving in the public sector? We were dissatisfied with much of the available literature in the field, which often seemed theoretical and abstract and far removed from the real world of public management. We wanted our students to see and experience the issues and the challenges that will face them in the public sector.

We share a strong belief in the value of a case study approach to teaching and use case studies extensively in our courses. We believe that only by putting our students in the shoes of real, hands-on public managers can we train them for successful public service careers. As a result, we decided that if this book was going to do what we hoped it would do, we needed to seek out successful leader-managers from a variety of policy areas, levels of government, regions of the country, and political backgrounds and ask them the kinds of questions that we and our students would ask them if they were in our classrooms.

Fortunately, we were able to convince seven outstanding leader-managers to be part of this effort. We went to each of them for in-person, in-depth interviews. We taped each interview and then culled through the transcripts, searching for common ground; and we found it. We identified six key skills and practices that all our leader-managers believed were important and that they attempted to apply in important positions of public responsibility. In the first part of the book, we discuss these skills in detail, using extended quotes from the interviews as well as our own words that reflect our experiences as leader-managers. The second part provides the interview transcripts themselves, giving readers a chance to explore the world of each leader-manager in depth.

For that reason our first and most important thanks go to the seven leader-managers who so generously gave of their time to us. Each provided a window on his or her world over a remarkably wide range of public responsibility, from running a busy state court system to leading troops in combat. Without them this book could not have happened, and to each we give our thanks: Kim Belshé, the secretary of the Health and Human Services Agency in California; John Catoe, the general manager of the Washington Metro transit system; Tom Payzant, the former superintendent of the Boston public schools and several other school systems across the country as well as assistant secretary in the U.S. Department of Education; Federico Peña, the former mayor of Denver and the secretary of two federal cabinet-level agencies; Mary Peters, the head of both the Arizona and the federal Department of Transportation; Jean Toal, the chief justice of the Supreme Court of South Carolina; and Bernard "Mick" Trainor, lieutenant general (ret.) in the United States Marine Corps.

We also want to acknowledge the staff at M.E. Sharpe for their support of this project and Harry Briggs, in particular, who has been unbelievably patient and supportive throughout the process. Harry provided encouragement and advice as we shaped our project, and he waited patiently as we extended our timeline to bring all the pieces together. Finally, we thank our families and loved ones, Kitty Dukakis and Meredith Montague in particular, who granted the extra hour and the extra day as we completed the interviews and crafted the final product.

LEADER-MANAGERS
in the
PUBLIC SECTOR

1

Leading and Managing in the Public Sector

The Leader-Manager

In America today the need for effective government has never been greater. At the local level, we want fire and police departments that can protect our property and us, and we demand schools that can provide quality education. From state government, we expect an efficient and well-maintained transportation system, equitable social services, effective higher education, and a safety net for the poor. From our national officials, we expect protection from foreign enemies, and we rely upon a number of programs to ensure our social and economic security.

We look to our government officials to meet these expectations, yet they often fall short. To some observers of the public sector, the critical need is for more effective *leadership*. From this perspective, we need individuals who can look at the "big picture" and lead others to overcome the challenges we all face. We want leaders with vision who can bring together resources and people to address our common concerns. We look for inspiration, integrity, and purpose in our government officials.

To other observers, the more important need is better *management*. From this perspective, the key concern is effective and efficient delivery of government services. We need government officials who are skilled in the allocation and oversight of personnel and financial resources. We need effective managers who can implement and deliver the many services that we expect from government at the lowest possible cost.

In fact, both are needed. Rather than a dichotomy between leadership and management, we need public servants who can effectively operate in both realms. We need *leader-managers* who demonstrate leadership as well as management skills. We need individuals who can bring vision to their work as well as organize resources to effectively deliver services. We need public sector leaders who can inspire others to address the challenges we face, who can be effective managers to implement government policies, and who can do both with a high degree of competence and absolute integrity.

The focus in this book on the leader-manager—one who has both formidable leadership *and* management skills—is not the typical starting point in the academic literature. Scholars in this area most often note the *differences* between leadership and management. John Kotter, for example, describes leadership as "the development of vision and strategies, the alignment of relevant people behind those strategies, and the empowerment of individuals to make the vision happen, despite obstacles" (1999, 10). Leadership is about establishing direction for an organization, then bringing together, motivating, and inspiring people to move in that direction (Kotter 1990). In contrast, Kotter notes that management "involves keeping the current system operating through planning, budgeting, organizing, staffing, controlling, and problem solving" (1999, 10). Management skills work through hierarchy and systems, rather than the people and culture that characterize the area of leadership.

Lee Bolman and Terrence Deal present a similar perspective. A leader, they insist, must have the "power" of a "warrior" and the "passion" of a "wizard." As a warrior, a leader must fight for an organization's agenda by building a "power base of allies, resources, networks, and coalitions." Leaders also are wizards who "bring imagination, insight, creativity, vision, meaning, and magic to the work of leadership." In contrast, managers operate from an "analyst" and "caregiver" perspective. As analysts, managers highlight "rationality, analysis, logic, facts, and data" (2006, 21). As caregivers, managers focus on people, relationships, and collaboration.

While highlighting these differences, scholars also note that the same individual often is challenged to be *both* a leader and a manager. Kotter, for example, refers to the "manager/leader" who must try to exercise the skills of both. Roy Williams and Terrence Deal conclude that successful organizations "need to develop a new brand of manager-leader; we crave people who have both feet on the ground as well as a lofty vision of the future" (2003, 8). Elliot Jaques and Stephen Clement go a step further, arguing that a distinction between leadership and management is not productive. As they conclude, "all managers carry leadership accountability" (1991, 8). Montgomery Van Wart, in his review of leadership studies, takes a similar position, noting that one of the "enormous challenges of great leadership is the seamless blending of the more operational-managerial dimensions with the visionary leadership functions" (2005, 25).

We agree with Van Wart: public servants today are called upon to be *both* leaders and managers. To be certain, there are differences between leadership and management. Leadership, as Kotter and others note, typically involves a long-term horizon, while management implies a short-term perspective. Leadership is often cast at a general level of motivating followers, while management highlights the immediate tasks required to meet specific goals. Leadership focuses on building a vision for the future, while management emphasizes the use of resources to meet organizational goals.

To focus on differences, however, obscures the important point that leader-managers must be effective in both domains. Kim Belshé, secretary of the California Health and Human Services Agency and one of our leader-managers interviewed for this project, captured this critical point:

> I see myself as a leader-manager. I view my role as being part leader and part manager. I work to find the reasonable and responsible middle ground between the two roles. It's not all big vision and articulation of where we need to go, and it's not all micromanagement. I have a responsibility to be clear as to where we need to go as an organization, but I also need to engage my staff colleagues in the "whys" that underpin our jobs as well as the "hows" of getting there. A leader-manager is someone who can lead the charge to advance the vision and goals.

One way to capture this perspective of a leader-manager is by a continuum, as in Figure 1.1, in which vertical lines at different points along the continuum indicate different combinations of leadership and management. On the left side of Figure 1.1 (at point A), for example, the combination leans to more leadership and less management. A leader-manager in this area would focus on key leadership tasks, such as developing the vision and direction for an organization or scanning the environment for long-term challenges. Managerial responsibilities continue, but the focus is on activities more commonly associated with leadership. In contrast, on the right side of Figure 1.1 (at point B), a leader-manager is more absorbed in the challenges of management. Directing the allocation of financial, personnel, and other resources to effectively implement a program might occupy most of a person's time. Leadership skills are still tested, but the emphasis is on managerial challenges.

Leader-managers can lie on different points on this continuum, representing different combinations of leadership and management challenges. Some of this variation can be attributed to the organizational position held by a leader-manager. An agency secretary or department head, for example, is in a position that typically carries heavy leadership demands. In contrast, a

Figure 1.1 **The Leader-Manager Continuum**

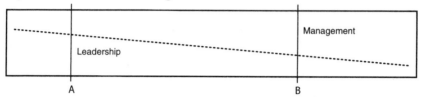

A   B

position near the middle or bottom of the organization is likely to involve more management activities. In a public school system, for example, a superintendent is typically further to the left on the continuum than a principal would be. A superintendent is concerned with long-term policy issues, while a principal is immersed in managing and operating an individual school. Still, the superintendent, despite a focus on leadership, must be attentive to the management activities that move the school system forward, and the principal plays a leadership role at the school level to provide general direction and guidance for teachers and others in the school community.

A leader-manager's placement on the continuum can vary for other reasons as well. For example, in the early days of a new gubernatorial administration, top leader-managers may focus on the leadership challenges of charting a new direction for an agency. At a later point, the focus might shift to managerial and implementation challenges. Variation is possible also simply by the skills and inclinations of an individual. Some people are more inclined to focus on typical leadership issues, while others prefer managerial challenges. This might be true even for leader-managers holding the same position in an organization. One school principal, for example, might focus energy on broad leadership activities, such as developing parent and community support, while another principal devotes more time to developing a class schedule and other administrative matters.

In short, leader-managers are *both* leaders and managers, albeit in different and varying combinations. Indeed, at different times, the same individual might utilize a different package of leadership and management skills. At one stage the ability to present a long-term vision, often associated with leadership, might be most important, but at another point organizational skills, often associated with management, become more critical. The bottom line: to be successful, a leader-manager must be effective in both domains.

These distinctions between leadership and management are important to note, but this project has pointed us in a different direction that emphasizes the *common practices* that are inherent in *both* leadership and management. That is, while leadership and management cover some different ground, they are both built upon a set of similar strategies and practices. Both leaders and managers, for example, must foster collaboration and support among key constituencies inside and outside the organization. Lacking such support, success of any kind is doubtful. Both leaders and managers must build effective organizations that can harness the creative skills of those who work in the organization. Designing an effective organization is a key practice for a leader-manager seeking organizational success.

The remainder of this book is focused on six common practices that constitute the foundation for an effective leader-manager. These practices are drawn from our interviews with leader-managers as well as our own experiences. The six practices are:

- *Picking and motivating your people*—One of the most important tasks of a leader-manager is hiring and motivating staff. Leader-managers need to build a team and develop a common vision that will guide the organization. They need staff that understands the organization's culture and environment. Leader-managers need to delegate to staff members while also mentoring them to achieve to their highest level.

- *Walking around . . . listening . . . learning*—Leader-managers need to spend time on the "factory floor" of the organization, learning about what makes the organization work and what can make it work better. They need to be excellent listeners, and they need to connect with their staff. They also need to take advantage of opportunities to learn more about their organization and the broader environment. Learning can take place in different venues, from informal conversations to formal coursework.

- *Fostering collaboration and support*—Building support for organizational goals among constituencies inside and outside the organization is critical to the success of a leader-manager. This requires effective communication that will foster relationships among key individuals and organizations. It requires consensus-building skills. Persistence and timing are important, along with understanding the self-interests of key collaborators.

- *Building effective organizations*—Leader-managers need to create organizations—and connections among organizations—that will support the achievement of goals. Lines of authority and communication within and across organizations play an important role in the effective delivery of services.

- *Communicating with the public*—Strategic communications with the public and other outside constituencies are important for an effective leader-manager. The media, in particular, play a key role in setting the public agenda. Strong and effective leader-managers will always face press criticism, but if they manage their media relations seriously and effectively, the media can become an ally in the achievement of organizational goals.

7

- *Demonstrating character and integrity*—Leader-managers are role models. Their words and actions exemplify success for others in the organization. The core values of leader-managers are important, as is their integrity in working with others inside and outside the organization.

Leader-managers face many challenges. Increasing public demands, which often conflict, combine with new technologies and an ever-changing social and economic environment to produce a complicated and often daunting agenda for public servants. To meet these challenges, leader-managers are needed who can develop the critical skills and competencies we have outlined. It is a career-long task, and mistakes will be made, but developing this skill set is critical for effective public servants at all levels of government.

The next chapter introduces seven leader-managers who demonstrate these key practices. The individuals we interviewed represent a range of experiences as leader-managers in the public sector. To these seven, we add our own experiences as additional examples of leader-managers. The chapters that follow provide details and examples of how these individuals demonstrated the common practices of an effective leader-manager. The final chapter offers a summary and reflection on the practices needed in the development of future leader-managers.

Introducing Our Leader-Managers

At the heart of this book are interviews conducted with seven leader-managers across the country. The chapters that follow draw heavily from these interviews; the complete transcripts of the interviews are included in the second half of the book. We chose the seven individuals based upon several criteria. We wanted representation from all levels of government, from different policy areas, from different regions of the country, and from different political persuasions. As Table 2.1 indicates, we achieved a fairly broad representation of interests and experiences. The remainder of this chapter briefly introduces each interviewee.

Kimberly Belshé is an accomplished leader-manager in the health care field at the state and federal levels of government. Born and raised in California, she traveled east to earn a bachelor's degree in government from Harvard University and a master's degree in public policy from Princeton University. Upon graduating in 1987, Belshé returned to California to work at the state level in a new welfare-to-work program called GAIN. After a relatively short time in Sacramento, she moved to San Francisco to work in the private sector at Ogilvy and Mather, a public affairs firm.

Belshé's interest in returning to the public sector led her back to the East Coast, to Washington, DC, where she served as a legislative assistant for California's U.S. Senator Pete Wilson. As a key assistant in health policy, Belshé expanded her experiences to include the legislative side of policy-making. Pete Wilson's gubernatorial victory sent her back to California as Wilson's deputy secretary in the Health and Welfare Agency, the predecessor to the agency she currently directs. Opportunities continued to open up. In 1993, at the age of

Table 2.1

Our Leader-Managers

	Level of government and position			Policy area	Geographic experience
	Local	State	Federal		
Kim Belshé		Secretary		Human services	California
John Catoe	General manager			Transportation	California; Washington, DC
Tom Payzant	Superintendent		Assistant secretary	Education	Massachusetts; California; Oklahoma; Washington, DC
Federico Peña	Mayor		Secretary	General government, transportation, energy	Colorado; Washington, DC
Mary Peters		Secretary	Secretary	Transportation	Arizona; Washington, DC
Jean Toal		Chief justice		Judiciary	South Carolina
Bernard Trainor			General	Military, journalism	Overseas; northeast states

thirty-three, Belshé stepped in as director of health services and continued to serve in that role until the end of the Wilson administration in 1999.

In November 2003, Belshé was appointed by Governor Arnold Schwarzenegger to serve as the secretary of the Health and Human Services Agency. As secretary, she oversees one of the largest agencies in California state government with 32,000 employees and a budget of more than $76 billion. She is a key adviser for the governor on a broad range of health and social service issues.

The health and social service policy arena is complicated and challenging. It has been a true test of Belshé's leadership and management skills. Perhaps most noteworthy was her role in bringing a major health-care reform package to the California legislature. Although ultimately unsuccessful in a very partisan and fiscally strained environment, this reform package required Belshé to foster collaboration among and support from key actors in the public, private, and nonprofit sectors. The failure to get final legislative approval was indicative of the politically charged nature of the health-care debate in California and nationwide.

John B. Catoe Jr. is a leader in the urban transportation arena and, like Belshé, has experience on both coasts. Catoe's childhood was spent in Washington, DC, where he lived in public housing and attended the DC schools. Leaving the East Coast, however, Catoe has spent much of his working career in California. He earned an undergraduate degree in business administration at the University of Redlands in Redlands, California, and then joined the Orange County Transit District in 1979 as an employee training and development administrator. He continued working for Orange County until 1996 when he became the director of transit services for the city of Santa Monica. In 1997 and 2000, the American Public Transportation Association recognized Santa Monica Transit Services as the number one transit agency in the nation. From 2000 to 2006, Catoe served as the deputy chief executive officer of the Los Angeles County Metropolitan Transportation Authority. In that capacity he had broad responsibility for transportation in California's largest city and its surrounding area.

From January 2007 to April 2010, Catoe served as the general manager of the Washington Metropolitan Area Transit Authority, commonly known as the DC Metro. As general manager, Catoe led the second largest rail transit system in the country and the fifth largest bus network. With over 10,000 employees and a $2.2 billion budget, the DC Metro plays a major role in shaping the local economy in the nation's capital.

Urban transportation systems pose major policy and administrative challenges for any leader-manager. Funded with a combination of user fees and public monies, urban transit systems often face budget deficits. In fact, Catoe became general manager of the Metro as it faced a $100 million shortfall. Furthermore, rail and bus services require careful oversight to maintain rider and employee safety as well as a minute-by-minute schedule for service delivery. Leader-managers in the urban transit world must build an organization with staff from the top to the bottom that can work together to meet these challenges

Thomas W. Payzant has been a leader in the education field for over forty years. He began his career as a social studies teacher in 1963 and completed graduate studies at Harvard University. After a short assignment in New Orleans, he started his first superintendency in Springfield Township in Pennsylvania, serving in that role from 1969 to 1973. Other superintendencies followed: Eugene, Oregon Public Schools (1973–1978), Oklahoma City Public Schools (1979–1982) and San Diego Unified School District (1982–1993).

In 1993, Payzant joined the Clinton administration as assistant secretary for elementary and secondary education. This experience at the federal level, which is the topic of discussion at several points during our interview, provided a quite different leader-manager experience in comparison to superintendencies of local school districts. However, Payzant's passion for leadership at the district level was piqued when the superintendency in Boston became available and he was actively courted for the job. Accepting the position, Payzant served as superintendent of the Boston Public Schools from October 1995 through June 2006. Since retiring from the Boston position, he has served as a senior lecturer in the Graduate School of Education at Harvard University.

In Boston, Payzant was the school system's first appointed superintendent under a new governance system in which the mayor appoints school committee (school board) members and, indirectly, the superintendent. Payzant's tenure as superintendent was a period of stability and gradual progress for the Boston schools. Payzant was widely noted for his consistent focus on teaching and learning and his efforts to raise academic achievement in the school system. He earned praise for his management and leadership skills in a challenging political environment. In 2004, he received the Richard B. Green Award in Urban Excellence from the Council of Great City Schools; in 2005, *Governing Magazine* named him one of eight "Public Officials of the Year"; and in 2006, the Boston Public Schools won the prestigious Broad Award for the best urban school system in the country.

In recent years public education, particularly in America's cities, has been one of the most challenging policy and administrative arenas. The somewhat insular world of the schoolhouse has been subject to growing demands for educational and fiscal accountability. The federal No Child Left Behind law, the Bush administration's version of the Elementary and Secondary Education Act, is the most recent accountability example; it calls for all students to achieve "proficiency" by 2014. School systems that fail to achieve the law's goals are subject to increasing levels of scrutiny and administrative change. For urban America, this rise in accountability has come at the same time as economic and demographic changes have left many cities with a diminished tax base, yet a larger minority, immigrant, and less affluent population. Urban schools—and their superintendents—are at the center of this very difficult environment. Superintendents like Tom Payzant are tested across the board in their leadership and management skills.

Federico Fabian Peña has had a distinguished career in public service at all three levels of government. He is a native of Texas, but moved to Denver as a civil rights lawyer and ran for the Colorado House of Representatives in 1978. He served four years in the House, where he rose to be the Democratic minority leader. In 1983, he defeated a mayoral incumbent to become Denver's first Hispanic mayor. He served two terms, leaving the mayor's office in 1991. He assisted in the transition process for newly elected President Clinton and was tapped by Clinton to be secretary of the U.S. Department of Transportation (DOT). He held that position from 1993 to 1997, than served a short period as secretary of the U.S. Department of Energy until 1998. Upon leaving the Clinton administration, he entered the private sector as a member and then managing director of Vestar Capital Partners, an investment firm. Our interview focused initially on his term as mayor, but the conversation soon included his experiences at the national level.

Being the mayor of a major city is one of the most challenging jobs in public service. Like Tom Payzant's description of life as an urban school superintendent, it is a 24/7 assignment. Mayors typically attend many public meetings and are in frequent contact with constituents and their own employees who deliver services throughout the city. Big-city mayors are tasked with providing vision and long-term direction for the city, while also being responsible for the day-to-day delivery of services. From infrastructure to social services to education, mayors are involved in a wide range of public sector activities. During Peña's tenure as mayor there were a number of major projects, including construction of one of the largest airports in the country. It is an intense job that tests the skills of the best leader-managers.

Mary E. Peters is a leader-manager in the transportation industry at the state and federal level. Her career began, however, in a much more modest way. Although a native of Arizona, she moved to Indiana with her young family and for fifteen years raised three children and worked in a variety of jobs, including day care, meatpacking, and tax preparation. She moved back to Arizona with her family and returned to school, graduating with a bachelor's degree from the University of Phoenix while starting her career at the Arizona

Department of Transportation in 1985. She worked her way up the career ladder, from contract administrator to deputy director for administration to deputy director and finally to director of the Arizona DOT in 1998. She served in that capacity for two years, then spent one year in the private sector as the senior vice president and national director of transportation policy and consulting at HDR Inc., an architectural, engineering, and consulting firm.

In 2001, Peters was appointed by President George W. Bush to serve as administrator of the Federal Highway Administration. She held this position through the first term of the Bush presidency. Acknowledging her work as a leader-manager, the Women's Transportation Seminar (WTS) recognized Peters as the 2004 International Woman of the Year and made her the first recipient of their Lifetime Achievement Award. In 2006, Peters became secretary of the U.S. Department of Transportation and served until the conclusion of the Bush administration in January 2009. She brought an inclusive management style to the federal DOT, as well as a strong belief in the role of private partners to address the needs of the transportation system.

Transportation policy poses many challenges for Mary Peters and other leader-managers. Among these challenges, funding is one of the most prominent. Building and maintaining the capital infrastructure while also meeting operating costs for various transportation modes, such as rail and highway, is very costly, leading to an important debate about the use of user fees and private partnerships as ways to reduce the demands on the public purse. The use and adaptation of new technologies is another important area. High-speed rail, for example, involves a variety of technological innovations necessary for upgrading and modernizing rail systems. Leader-managers face these and other issues as they attempt to bring coherency and coordination to a complex, multimodal system that seeks to serve the many transportation needs of the nation.

Jean Hoefer Toal's rise to be chief justice of the South Carolina Supreme Court was preceded by twenty years as an attorney and legislator. After graduating from the University of South Carolina Law School in 1968, Toal began a career in private practice during which she engaged in a mix of plaintiff and defense work, criminal trial work, and constitutional litigation. While practicing law, she was elected to the South Carolina House of Representatives. Elected six times to that body, she became a legislative leader in constitutional law and state finances while chairing several committees and leading floor debate and legislative change in a variety of areas, including criminal and corporate law, workers' compensation, structure of the court system, environmental law, utilities regulation, and rules reform of the legislature itself.

In 1988, Toal was elected by her colleagues in the legislature to serve on the South Carolina Supreme Court. South Carolina is one of the few states in which justices of the supreme court are selected by a vote of the state legislature. In 2000, she was picked by the legislature to complete the term of the retiring chief justice of the supreme court, then in 2004 she was elected by the legislature again for her own ten-year term as chief justice. She has the distinction of being the first woman on the South Carolina Supreme Court and the first female chief justice of that court.

As leader-manager and chief administrator of the state court system, Toal has been particularly attuned to issues of technology and gender. One of her key initiatives as court administrator has been expanded use of technology throughout the court system. Moving to a web-based tracking system has allowed courts in rural and less affluent areas of the state to significantly increase their productivity and effectiveness in responding to the increasing workload of cases. Equally important is Toal's attention to matters of gender. Having built her career in a profession dominated by males, Toal considers the mentoring of women and underrepresented groups a central part of her role as a leader-manager. As she says, it is very important for leader-managers to "let the ladder down" and help those building their careers in a world in which gender and racial bias still exist.

From private practice, to the legislature, to the supreme court, Justice Toal has made her mark on South Carolina. As one U.S. circuit judge commented, "Jean Toal has to be recognized as the most important female in the last century in the state of South Carolina."

Bernard E. Trainor is an accomplished leader-manager with experience in the military, journalism and higher education. Known to many as Mick, he joined the Marine Corps in 1946 and served with distinction for thirty-nine years. He received numerous awards and citations for combat service in Korea and Vietnam as well as peacetime assignments, including military instructor and director of recruitment in the northeastern United States. He retired in 1985 with the rank of lieutenant general.

Upon retiring Trainor joined the *New York Times* as a military correspondent. He traveled widely around the world, reporting on military activities, including the Iran-Iraq War in the late 1980s. In 1990, he began a six-year tenure as the director of the National Security Program at Harvard University's Kennedy School of Government. In his postmilitary career, Trainor also turned to writing, producing two books with Michael Gordon. *The Generals' War: The Inside Story of the Conflict in the Gulf* was published in 1995 and quickly became an acclaimed account of the Gulf War. A second book, *Cobra II: The Inside Story of the Invasion and Occupation of Iraq*, was published in 2006 and provided another detailed look at a major U.S. military operation.

More so than most policy areas, the military operates in a hierarchical fashion in which rank establishes, by definition, a chain of command that fundamentally shapes the world of a leader-manager. Leader-managers in the military have established assignments that delineate their general responsibilities for supervising those below in rank and following the orders of those above. However, even within this hierarchy the world of a leader-manager can vary. As Trainor points out, leadership in combat calls for a high level of inspiration that will convince soldiers to risk their lives in the heat of battle, whereas leadership in a non-combat situation is less intense and involves persuasion and other interpersonal strategies. In both, as he emphasized, the development of good interpersonal skills is critical.

The seven individuals introduced in this chapter provide the heart of our study. Each brings a different set of experiences and perspectives to the challenges of leading and managing in the public sector, although they also share some important common practices about what makes for an effective leader-manager. Discussion of those common practices, such as fostering collaboration and building effective organizations, forms the remaining chapters of our book.

Before proceeding to those chapters, however, we will introduce ourselves. We did not interview ourselves for this project, but our experiences and perspectives on public leadership and management inform and shape the text that follows. As one might guess, our experiences are at rather different levels of leadership and management, but as with our interviewees, there is common ground as well.

Michael S. Dukakis is best known as the presidential nominee of the Democratic Party in 1988, but he had a long career in Massachusetts politics prior to this campaign. He started in elected office as a town meeting member in his home community of Brookline, a suburb of Boston. After two years at the local level, in 1962 he won a seat in the Massachusetts House of Representatives. He served as a state representative for eight years before joining Boston's mayor, Kevin White, to run on the state Democratic Party ticket as lieutenant governor. When this ticket was defeated at the polls, he practiced law for two years, than threw his hat in the ring to run for governor. Successful this time, Dukakis served as governor of the Commonwealth from 1975 to 1979.

His reelection bid in 1978 was cut short by defeat in the Democratic primary by Edward King. This rebuke by his party carried with it some important lessons for Dukakis as a leader-manager, particularly in the area of coalition building. In 1982, he launched a rematch with King that ended in success in the primary and in the general election against the Republican Party nominee. A successful reelection effort in 1986 allowed Dukakis to serve two full terms in the 1980s.

Reflecting on his years as governor, Dukakis notes that picking excellent people for key positions is as important as anything a leader-manager does in the public sector. Further, one lesson that was indelibly etched on his brain after twelve years as governor was that leading and managing in the public sector is all about building coalitions. Unfortunately, a lot of people who seek to serve in public life do not understand that, and they invariably come to grief, no matter how successful they have been in other walks of life.

After the 1988 presidential run and completing his third term as governor in January 1991, Dukakis joined the faculty of Northeastern University as a Distinguished Professor in Political Science. He continues to teach in public administration and public policy at Northeastern as well as UCLA.

John Portz brings a leader-manager perspective from the middle ranks of a university and the local political level. After attending college in Wisconsin, Portz joined Northeastern University in 1988 as an assistant professor in the Department of Political Science. He taught in the areas of state and local government as well as public administration, while conducting research in economic development and education. In 2001, he began an administrative career, first as the director of the university honors program, then as chair of his department. In both roles, he supervised a three-person staff and worked with many other faculty, administrators, and students at the university.

Beyond academia, Portz participated in local, part-time politics in his home community of Watertown, a suburb of Boston. He lost his first election bid as a town councilor in 1995, but won subsequent elections, serving on the Town Council until 2005, when he successfully ran for the school committee (school board). He continues to serve in that capacity.

Although his experiences differ significantly from those of Dukakis, Portz concurs with the importance of coalition building as a key strategy for a successful leader-manager. Of particular note is the challenge of motivating others to help develop and implement a common agenda. As a university department head, Portz cajoles and encourages independent-minded faculty to support university and departmental initiatives, and as a local politician, he works with his elected colleagues, who also are quite independent-minded, to build coalitions to support policies and programs for the town and schools.

3

Picking and Motivating Your People

One of the best leader-managers we have ever known used to say that there were only three important things in managing in the public sector—people, people, and people.

Of course, he would have been the first to say that there are other factors that determine whether or not leader-managers succeed, but we cannot exaggerate the importance of putting together a team of dedicated public servants, motivating them to do great things, mentoring them as they develop their own capacity to lead, and getting the results that are expected of each.

John Catoe was explicit and eloquent on the subject as he described taking over the Washington Metro: "The first thing I did was assess the existing management team. Individually, and as a group, I looked at the areas with a lack of performance and also successful performance. There was only one area that I would rate at the top, and that was security and law enforcement. A top-notch person handled this area really well. I started looking at other people and the issues. We had two members of the executive team whom the board had influence in appointing, and they were awful. I made it clear with the board in my contract and in discussions that that's my job. You hold me accountable for the staff. They work for me, not for you."

It is hard to exaggerate the importance of that commitment from the board or the manager to whom you report. There is nothing wrong with suggestions or referrals from your board, legislators, politicians generally, or an elected chief executive. Good leader-managers should welcome suggestions from anyone and everyone who can help identify good people, but you should never concede the right or authority of anyone to tell you whom to hire or fire. Unless you have a clear understanding of that fundamental principle with the people to whom you report, you should not take the job in the first place.

The reason for that is clear. You are going to be held accountable for your performance. It would be embarrassing, to put it mildly, to have to explain your mistakes because the person who messed up under you was forced on you by somebody else. Do not ever let that happen. It has been the ruination of a lot of very good leader-managers.

How, then, did Catoe make his assessment of the people he inherited, particularly the two who were hired with board influence? "I based my assessment on their performance in the areas in which they were responsible. It was not just my assessment. It was the assessment of the rest of the management team and outsiders who work with them. 'We can't get anything from them. We never get an answer. Nothing happens. They offer great talk and concepts, but there's no implementation.' I fired them both."

Hiring the people who will work with and for you—building a team—is important at any level of an organization. A leader-manager has a host of issues to consider. Certainly, the expertise and experience of an applicant are important. Does the person have the skills needed to perform the job? Equally important, if not more so, are the attitude and approach that applicants bring to the job. What level of energy and passion do they bring to the workplace?

John Catoe placed the highest regard on this second set of qualities. As Catoe said: "When I talk to people who work for me, I want to feel passion for what they do. I have thirty years of experience. If someone tells me he has thirty years experience, I'm not impressed. In fact, that could be a negative. Why are you at that level with thirty years experience? Are they willing to go through a process? Are they willing to take risks? Can they say, 'I know we do it this way, but I think we should try this.' When I hear that, I light up, and I appoint those people even though they might not be the most senior. They demonstrate the most passion and willingness to try something different."

"I look for commitment," Catoe emphasized. "I don't care what kind of background they have. I don't want a human resources expert who tells me, 'You can't do that.' I want someone who is going to look at it from the perspective of how we make this a great place for employees. What are the things we need to do from that perspective? It's the driver who drives the bus faithfully and speaks to the customers to start a relationship. It's the person who wants to make a train a little bit cleaner who is going to make this a great organization. And it's the supervisor who understands that her role isn't to write someone up but to help the system and the service operate correctly. That's what's going to make the agency great, and that's what we're going to focus on. I'm looking for people who understand that."

Note that Catoe is not looking for yes-men. He wants people who are willing to challenge the status quo and to challenge him. Mick Trainor felt the same way about a young officer who ultimately achieved great things in his military career. "You can give an order in the military," Trainor noted, "and obviously nobody is going to say 'no'; they'll say 'Aye, aye, sir.' They're going to do it, but with a level of enthusiasm that depends upon how you present it. At the same time you have to encourage people who disagree with you to speak up before you make a decision and frequently save you from your own folly. One of my company commanders in Vietnam was Tony Zinni. He was not shy about arguing with me. It didn't hurt him; he went on to four stars and became a theater commander."

People skills are often the most important quality you need to look for in identifying a good employee, particularly if you are hiring at a senior level. Michael Dukakis faced a major hiring challenge at the start of his second term as governor when the Massachusetts Department of Revenue came under heavy fire for poor performance and public charges of corruption. Dukakis took quick action by appointing a task force of experts under the leadership of a distinguished professor of tax law at Boston College Law School. The task force came back with a series of hard-hitting and timely recommendations for improving the department's performance.

The most important outcome was appointment of a new revenue commissioner who was not a tax expert, but a superb general manager with a flair for the dramatic. Ira Jackson might not have been able to balance his own checkbook, but he understood what it took to revive and reinspire a dispirited public agency. Jackson spent enormous amounts of time getting to know his career employees and learning from them. He used the media brilliantly to restore public confidence in the department, and he turned it into one of the best of its kind in the country.

Tom Payzant also saw the value in hiring top staff with good people skills. Payzant was a native of Massachusetts, but much of his professional career was spent in teaching and major administrative positions a long way from Massachusetts, including as superintendent of the San Diego schools and as assistant secretary of elementary and secondary education in the Clinton administration. As head of the public school system in Boston, however, he had the good sense to pick Michael Contompasis, the highly respected, longtime headmaster of Boston's fabled Boston Latin High School as his chief operating officer.

Contompasis was a good administrator and knew the system, but equally important he had a unique relationship with a number of key city politicians. Under Boston's mayor-appointed school-board system, the mayor and city council played a significant role in school politics. As Payzant tells the story: "The city council was like having another school board, reviewing budgets and other aspects of the schools. With respect to the council, Mike Contompasis was a great help. We developed a great partnership. For most of our tenure, there were anywhere between three and five members of the [thirteen-member] city council who came from Boston Latin. To these councilors, Mike was still the headmaster. We did a 'good cop, bad cop' routine. It made it a lot easier."

Federico Peña faced the problem of picking his key people at a unique moment in his mayoral effort in Denver—after a successful grassroots campaign with literally dozens and dozens of eager supporters anxious to be part of a young and exciting new administration. Peña had leadership experience in the Colorado legislature but, like most newly elected political chief executives, had never run anything remotely resembling the government of a major western city.

"The nature of my campaign was grassroots-based," Peña noted, "very optimistic and youth oriented; we attracted a lot of very talented professionals. I had to figure out a way to bring on board the right people. I wanted people who shared my values, and I wanted people who could work together. I didn't want prima donnas. I didn't want people who were going to be mistreating citizens, or people with a tough edge who were going to rub people the wrong way. I believed in bringing people together."

Peña sought a diverse group of individuals. "During my campaign gays got involved; labor was involved; all kinds of people were working together who never did before. I wanted my team to have that philosophy; we had to bring everybody together and work as a team. I wanted the government to reflect the entire city as it had not previously."

As in all new administrations, some of his choices were stars, and some were not. Some people just did not work out for him, and like many new leader-managers, Peña was reluctant to replace them. "I had a tendency," he says, "to give people a second chance or even a third chance. I think more experienced managers will tell you that if you have someone who is not working out, you probably need to make a quick change."

In picking your people it is very important to control the process. After all, your performance depends on it. Beware of "blue ribbon selection committees" and "national searches." There is nothing wrong with spreading your net far and wide, but understanding the local political culture and building effective coalitions are very, very important. Bringing in somebody who is unfamiliar with the local political environment can often be disastrous. Moreover, making fundamental change takes time. Unless new people from a thousand miles away have a real commitment to sticking with their job for an extended period of time, they will never get the job done.

That does not mean that prospective hires must have lived in the particular jurisdiction all their lives and intend to stay there indefinitely, but it helps. John Catoe had spent most of his career in California, but he was born and brought up in the District of Columbia, and those ties and associations were very helpful to him as he took on his new job.

Good leader-managers try to blend a combination of old and new into their staffs—grizzled veterans who still have energy and commitment with young people who possess zest and enthusiasm but with the sense and sensitivity to understand that policy analysis by itself does not achieve anything. It is people and coalition-building skills that make the difference.

There are at least four principal components in picking key staff: (1) defining the job; (2) spreading the net to identify candidates; (3) checking out prospects thoroughly, including tax and field checks; and (4) interviewing the candidate. Each component is critical. Without a clear definition and understanding of the responsibilities in a position, you are handicapped from the start. Beyond typical advertising, use your own networks to help identify the best candidates. When you have the list of candidates, review them thoroughly, including in the context of their place of work and home. A failure to do that can lead to disastrous results. Finally, the interview is important, too. Has the candidate done his homework? Does he have clear and well-informed ideas about why he wants the job and what he intends to do when he gets there? What are his weaknesses, and how will he or the leader-manager compensate for them? How well does he know the political culture?

People, people, people—a great team makes a leader-manager great. Just one weak link can make your life miserable.

Leader-managers do not just hire people and turn them loose. They do everything they can to motivate and help them succeed. A key step in that regard is building and supporting a vision for the organization. Every organization has a vision or mission that defines its role and, importantly, connects employees to the organization. It is difficult to imagine dedicated, motivated employees when an organization lacks a purpose or direction. A vision or mission offers a roadmap for all to follow.

As superintendent of schools in Boston, Tom Payzant established a vision and focus on "teaching and learning" as the core element in school reform. He knew that inspiring teachers and administrators in the school system required a vision that could be sustained and supported over a period of years. As he noted: "It is critical to get clarity around a few key goals, stick with them, and then have a plan for doing work that will be coherent. I knew there would be many distractions in Boston. The only way I could really offset that was to have a plan that was tight, focused, and relentless."

Under Payzant's leadership, in 1996 the Boston Public Schools developed a five-year plan known as Focus on Children. Renewed in 2001, the central element in the plan was a clear and consistent focus on "teaching and learning." For any initiative or proposal that came forward, the question was: "How did it support improved teaching and learning?" In meetings with staff, media, parents, and the general public, this became the consistent frame of reference.

A vision provides direction, which is critical in motivating members of an organization to contribute at their highest level. Payzant knew that not only would he face many pressures and demands, but that teachers and administrators in the school system also would face multiple demands on their time. This swirl of pressures and activities can easily overwhelm anyone in an organization, leading to a dissipation of effort and work. People in the organization begin to ask, "Why are we doing this?" "Is this important?" A vision and focus on the core purpose of an organization play a key role in minimizing such distractions and inspiring and sustaining employees in their work.

For Mary Peters, establishing such a vision was a key part of her role as a leader-manager in the transportation industry. From her days in the Arizona Department of Transportation, Peters noted the critical importance of giving employees a sense of direction. "You hire good, qualified people," Peters emphasized; "then you put them into positions of responsibility and let them do their job. But the most important thing you have to do is to give them a sense of direction. Where are we going? What is it we need to accomplish at the end of the day?"

"Employees need to have a sense of where we're going and why," Peters noted. "For example, when we had a new hire in the contracts office, I'd check a car out of the motor pool, and we would drive around and look at DOT projects. I'd say, 'This is what you're doing. You're delivering transportation projects for the people of Arizona. You're not just negotiating a contract or monitoring a contract or writing an RFP [request for proposals]; you're delivering a transportation system.' People need to see what they're doing."

The work that is done across an organization needs to be connected to the overall goals and vision. That is how you get everybody on board and capture the collective wisdom of the organization. At the U.S. Department of Transportation, Peters emphasized the process of connecting employees to the goals of the department. "We usually talked to people in small groups. We talked to people across the organization as well as down into the organization. We talked about the three priority areas—safety, overall performance, twenty-first century solutions—and developed them into action plans. We wanted to make sure that everyone contributed in some way. You go down, across, and up and down, communicating with everybody in the organization."

"I call it the 'line of sight' issue," Peters continued. "No matter where anyone is in the U.S. DOT, as big and as complex as we are, they have to have a 'line of sight' between what they are doing on a day-to-day basis and what it is we're trying to accomplish as an organization. If they can't see that, they don't understand what they're working for. They need to know, 'This is the end-game. This is where we're going. This is your role, your contribution to doing that.' That's how you tap into the collective wisdom. You let people know where you're going. You ask them to help define how to get there. You use their background. You involve them and you reward them."

For our leader-managers, a vision is not an abstraction that exists somewhere separate from the organization. People are motivated when they can see the connection between their work and the purpose of the unit. Mick Trainor, operating in a military environment, pushed to keep a focus on the key tasks of the organization: "When I was the Marine Corps deputy to the Joint Chiefs of Staff, some issues were very complicated and politically sensitive. I would bring action officers in and they would talk about the problems and go on and on. I said, 'What's the issue?' I'd ask for a point paper, and I would get pages of nonsense. I'd say, 'Point papers are no more than one page, double-spaced.' And then I had a sign made up and framed for my office. It said: 'Issue: What is the issue that is important? What are we trying to do?' That's what I did when I went into the First Marine Corps District in New York on my recruiting assignment. 'What are we trying to do? Don't tell me what we're doing; tell me what it is we want to do and then we'll figure out how to do it.'"

Creating a "line of sight" for people who work with and for you is part of empowering them to contribute to the overall mission of the organization. Also important is recognizing the interests and goals of each employee and aligning those with the goals of the organization. In a university setting, John Portz considers this alignment one of his important tasks as a department chair. He tries to understand the goals of each member of the faculty and staff, and then helps to connect those to the goals of the unit. If a member of the faculty is interested in the broad impacts of the war in Iraq on democratization in other countries, for example, helping to develop a speakers' series meets that interest while serving the educational and research goals of the department and the university.

Creating these connections and building a vision and sense of purpose in an organization require clear, consistent communication. John Catoe emphasized the importance of communication with workers in the Washington Metro: "There is a minimum weekly, and sometimes three times a week, memo from me as an e-mail to every employee in this agency. There are 10,000 employees. Every event that occurs, our employees know about it before it gets to the newspaper. Every time we have a board meeting, I tell them what's going to the board. After the meeting, they'll know exactly what the board did. When we have shifts in the organization, they know about it beforehand. The funding issues, they know about them. For the layoffs we had to do, I must have had fifteen meetings with employees to say, 'Here is where we are; here are the steps; here is what will happen to those individuals who are laid off.' I did this not only verbally but also in writing. We took care of them, not only from the standpoint of severance, but we walked them through the process of the transition."

Weekly memos and other forms of communication help employees to be part of an organization. Two-way lines of communication are created that help employees become vested in the future of the organization. As Catoe pointed out, however, leader-managers must listen to what they hear, and take action. "It's easy to listen. The key is you'd better enact some of those things you hear about. You've got to come right back and get your managers together. Tell them, 'Jim, I want this done and I want this done. I want to fix it.' When employees see that, they talk to you and action occurs, then they'll start talking to you more. You're beginning a process now. They're giving you feedback. You know things can happen. I get dozens of e-mails. I give out my e-mail to employees directly."

This becomes part of the learning process discussed in the next chapter. Communication and feedback become the norm in this culture. Members of an organization strive to excel. As Catoe concluded: "It isn't me going in and doing everything; it's me creating the environment in which people can perform. I fundamentally believe that people come to work to do a good job. They don't wake up in the morning thinking how bad they can be today. I identify people who I think have high potential, and I put them in jobs of responsibility. I listen to the input they give me in making decisions. I don't just listen to my managers. I go out and talk to people. I talk to the mechanics and other workers, including supervisors, because these are the people who can tell you what's going on."

It is also important for leader-managers to mentor others in the organization and in public service generally. Jean Toal on the South Carolina Supreme Court saw mentoring as one of her major responsibilities. "I didn't have a strong mentoring network when I came through. There were so few women. I had my classmates who believed in me, and some people in the initial law firm I went to. But it was hard for a young woman to get started in the law business."

"I think it is important," said Toal, "particularly for people not in the mainstream, to be mentored. I spend a lot of time with new judges, and I get other senior and experienced judges to do the same. I have a very formal program for new judges. I have them meet with a group of senior judges, not just one, so they get different perspectives."

For Toal, mentoring goes beyond judges in the court system. She explained:

"We've also started something called the Chief Justice's Commission on the Profession. It's a group of really bright lawyers, judges, and professors from all over the state who meet to discuss ways to improve the image of the profession and the values of the profession. They come up with good ideas all the time. The most recent one is to start a mentoring program for new lawyers. We have so many young lawyers who get in trouble their first couple of years. Often, it's because they don't feel like they have anybody they can turn to."

"Another group that I think mentoring is extremely important for is women," Toal noted. "We didn't have a South Carolina Women Lawyers Association when I first started. But we have a very vibrant Women Lawyers Association now, and over time, we've developed a culture among the women of helping each other out and reaching down to those who need a little help or push to be successful. My mantra is 'Keep the ladder down.' There's a great tendency among some trailblazers to keep their story of how they made it to themselves. Some leaders think, 'If I let too many people in on this, then I won't get where I want to go.' That's terrible, in my view. What you need to do is leave the ladder down and pull the next group up the ladder. I say that so often that the South Carolina Women Lawyers Association finally created a small pin with a ladder and a little South Carolina wren climbing up the ladder. They call it Toal's Ladder Pin."

"As you become successful," Toal concluded, "it's awfully important to let somebody else get in on whatever kind of a little aura you have that they could use. I remember the years when I didn't have any of that aura. I would look with envy at the people who had made it, and I would think, 'How can I get there?' It's so easy if you have had some success in life to let somebody else share that reflected glory."

Mary Peters highlighted the importance of mentoring as well. "You want to grow that next generation of leaders. At the Arizona DOT, for people who reported directly to me, I required that they mentor someone else, hopefully three other people. The organization was so white, male-centric. At least one of those three needed to be a woman or minority; we were just so under-represented in management by women and minorities. I think we have the responsibility to mentor people in the organization and to bring them along. It's a key responsibility of ours."

All of our leader-managers share a pride in public service and a strong desire to develop new leader-managers who share that pride and can go on to successful careers of their own. "When I think about our legacy," Kim Belshé of California's Health and Human Services Agency said, "certainly I hope there are legislative accomplishments over time and policy accomplishments as well. But I would hope that at the end of my tenure I can point to people accomplishments as well. I'm referring to my ability, and my team's ability, to recruit and retain really smart and dedicated people, from senior managers to [young] people in our executive fellows program. When we get a good person in the agency, we need to talk with him or her about the future. Tell them: 'Don't run off to law school or some other graduate program just yet. Let's see if we can find a job in state service to give you more exposure to public policy.'"

John Catoe felt the same way about Washington Metro. "I enjoy sitting back and watching people be great. It's like a teacher who sees his students go off and succeed. The students may not ever send a note, but you can see that you were involved in having that happen. That needs to happen here. When I leave, I want this to be a great organization. That's the reward I want. That's what I will feel good about. I came here because I love to fix stuff. My success is that when I leave, this system is far better than what it is now. And there are good people and good managers in place. There are good managers who are going to keep it that way. Then I'm happy. I'm ready to step away and say, 'Now, here it is.' And then people run the system. I don't need my name on the wall anywhere or pictures of me hanging in buildings."

Indeed, picking and motivating staff are absolutely critical functions. In the end, a leader-manager is only as good as the people who work for him or her in the organization. Picking the right people is the critical first step, but then motivating and inspiring them to achieve their best are equally important. Everyone needs that "line of sight" to connect to the organization, and they need support and mentorship to reach personal and organizational goals. As part of putting the right people in place, you also listen to others and learn more about the organization. The next chapter is devoted to that important practice.

4

Walking Around . . .
Listening . . . Learning

Picking and motivating competent and worthy staff are certainly critical first steps for any leader-manager, but equally important is to start the process of walking around, listening, and learning. A leader-manager "walks around" to hear from and inspire those in the field; he listens to others in order to better understand the needs of the organization; and he is constantly learning to develop his own skills and to enhance the effectiveness of the organization.

Managing by walking around should be an essential part of any leader-manager's life, but walking around by itself is not the whole story. If the leader-manager does not listen as he walks around, and if he does not respond effectively to what he is hearing, then showing up from time to time so his employees can see him will have little or no effect on his agency's performance.

Almost all of our leader-managers walk around—and they listen and learn from the experience. In fact, Tom Payzant made it an essential part of his workweek, and he did not do it just once. During his first year, he visited each of the 125 schools in the Boston school system. Thereafter, he made a point of visiting sixty to seventy schools each year, or about two per week. At first his visits were announced in advance, but after a few weeks, he made it clear that they would be spontaneous and unannounced. Any superintendent of schools knows that if you visit a school and announce it ahead of time, you probably will not see the school as it really is. Noted Payzant: "I didn't want special preparations made for the visits. I wanted to see what was going on under normal circumstances."

Of course, that can bother a lot of principals and teachers because they think the superintendent is trying to catch them napping. There are, of course, many occasions when your visit can and should be announced in advance, even if that means you are getting a scrubbed-up version of what goes on in the school every day. But Payzant wanted to listen, observe, and learn.

"My activities evolved over time," Payzant noted, "to where I wanted to get deeper into the teaching and learning work. I would spend more time in a few classrooms. The principal would often come with me. That was fine. I wanted to see what they were seeing. It was important to work with principals to help them understand what good instruction looked like.

"You have to know the work to lead the work. Part of knowing the work is seeing the work that is being done and that you think should be done . . . and what you can learn from what you see or hear. The 'walking around' allows you to do that. It also challenges the traditional view that superintendents sit in their offices and don't really know what the real world of schools is like."

Walking around is an important way to connect with staff in an organization. "It is about relationship building" Payzant emphasized. "The superintendent, like any leader who is removed from day-to-day contact with the work, can develop a mystique that separates him or her from what is happening in schools where the teaching and the learning work is done. You can become a distant name and title at the central office or on the six o'clock news, or a story in the *Globe* [the local newspaper]. But if you visit the schools, I don't care how big the system is, the word does get around. I had a master key, so I didn't have to ring the bell. The whispers would start: 'The superintendent is here.' It amazed me during my school visits throughout my career how many teachers would say, 'You are the first superintendent to come to my classroom.'"

Walking around and listening can also be wonderfully energizing after hours and days of doing other things. "If I was tired and frustrated by tough issues at school headquarters or city hall," Payzant noted, "I would go out to a school, and I would get pumped up. It reenergized me. You have to see the kids and see the people who are doing the work. One of the biggest challenges in urban America is creating a sense of hope that you can make a difference for children in an urban school system."

He did not listen just to principals and teachers. He would talk to students, too. "I can get a good sense of a school's climate just by walking around and watching what they are doing. I'd ask students, 'What are you doing today?' They would respond, 'I'm working on this. I've been in this small group today talking about this assignment.' Or I would go into another classroom and hear 'more worksheets.' You have to talk to the kids."

Mick Trainor took the same approach when he was given responsibility for military recruitment in the northeastern part of the country. "After I found out where my desk was," Trainor declared, "I went out and started to visit all the recruiting stations and the substations. I would talk to the NCOs [noncommissioned officers] and the regional officers who oversaw them. I would go myself and talk to the recruiters along with my senior NCO in my headquarters. We talked to the recruiters and to their wives. The wives are living out in the economy and trying to make ends meet. They're young. They have children, and they rarely see their husbands. Both are stressed. Some wives were working, so sometimes I'd hold meetings in the evening or at breakfast in the morning. The wives were very, very unhappy. I was a villain. I was the guy making demands on them. They complained about never seeing their husbands and that their husbands were always unhappy. They were afraid that in some instances their spouses were turning to the bottle.

"There wasn't much I could do about domestic problems," Trainor noted, "but the wives were able to vent and learn that somebody cared for their welfare and was trying to make things better. Last October, I ran into the wife of a recruiter who had served in Hartford. In the course of the conversation she told me how much she and other wives appreciated those little get-togethers. Imagine that—thirty-some odd years later she still remembered. The only way you're going to find out something about your organization is to go down to the factory floor, which is what I did."

Trainor visited all but one of the forty to forty-five recruiting stations and substations under his control. He never visited Presque Isle, Maine, however. "We never saw the recruiter who was up there. He was a sergeant, and the rumor was that he was married to an Indian and lived in a tepee. He was a guy who always had success, but he never made a single monthly quota. He made his quota of recruits after potato-picking season in Maine. When the winter weather turned snowy and cold, he would show prospects pictures of sunny South Carolina and Parris Island. That was the sort of creative recruiting I was looking for."

Walking around and listening was a critically important part of John Catoe's workday at the Washington Metro, and he insisted that his executive team do it, too. "When I arrived," Catoe said, "I told my executive team, 'You're going to ride the system. When you ride it this week, you're going to walk up to the first Metro employee you see and ask them how things are going.' Our legal counsel said, 'They're not going to want us to do that. They're going to ask, Who are these people?' But that's what we're going to do."

"At the next meeting," Catoe noted, "our legal counsel was shocked when she talked to the employee. 'The person thanked me for speaking to him and appreciated that I was using the system. Then, he proceeded to start telling me stuff.' That's now becoming a natural part of the executive team. At every meeting, members of the team report on what they learned while riding the system. That's going to become part of their direct reports. Pretty soon it starts spreading in the organization."

Catoe himself rode the system virtually every day. "Ninety-nine percent of the time I ride the system going to and from work. Whenever I arrive at a station, I always go to the station manager and shake his or her hand and ask how things are going. I also look for employees of the agency, such as the person cleaning the station, or a mechanic who's waiting for an assignment. I just go up and talk to them, asking questions. They give me incredible feedback about different issues and processes."

Catoe provided an example: "One station manager told me about a case where the work group came to replace tiles on one level in the station. The station manager approached the crew and said he had a similar problem downstairs. The operations guy said he doesn't have a work order for downstairs. So he comes back a week later just to replace the tiles downstairs. This process is wrong. We rate a manager on how many work orders he gets, versus the outcome. What's the outcome from a system standpoint? . . . I got that from talking to people."

Elected officials also engage in walking around, although the "factory floor" might look a little different. Indeed, an electoral campaign is all about meeting voters and listening to their concerns and issues. Once in office, meeting and listening to voters—now constituents—remain very important. For a governor like Michael Dukakis, "walking around the state," sometimes literally, becomes an important practice.

Dukakis involved his cabinet in this process, just as Catoe required his senior managers to ride the Washington Metro. In Dukakis's case, the entire cabinet and senior staff would travel to different regions of the state, at least once or twice a year, to listen. They would spend two or three days in each region holding cabinet meetings and meeting with political, civic, business, and community leaders. They solicited input and shared their goals and aspirations with the people of those regions on their turf, not in offices in the state capital. They obtained invaluable information and input that helped to shape policies and programs when they returned to the State House.

Even state chief justices "walk around" and listen. "I'm on the road a lot," Jean Toal said. "Fortunately, South Carolina is a small state, and Columbia is very central. You can be any place in South Carolina in three hours or less. So I get in my red van and drive all over the place. If we're about to initiate a technology program in a county, I tell people, 'Let's set up a meeting with your county council, and let me appear and publicly advocate for it.' When we complete a program in a county, I always make another appearance before the county council. I'm there simply to praise all the people. I get as personal as I can and praise the council . . . and give them a stake in the action. I travel widely to solicitors' meetings, public defenders' meetings, clerk of court meetings and others."

If walking around and listening are going to be effective, three things must happen. First, the leader-manager must be a good listener. That is not easy. Most of us in public life love to talk and express our ideas. We are great transmitters but often not very good receivers. Listening has important virtues. You save a lot of energy by not constantly talking at people and, instead, listening to what they have to say. Also, you learn things. When then-Senator Joseph Biden rode the Amtrak train from Wilmington to Washington, DC, every day, he learned a lot from the engineers, conductors, and his fellow passengers. That was one of the reasons he was a leading supporter of Amtrak in Congress and cosponsor of bills to invest serious money in its equipment and infrastructure.

Second, the leader-manager must walk around on a regular, ongoing basis. It cannot be a one-time event. If it is, employees will quickly understand that it is only for show, not for substance. Tom Glynn, the general manager of the metropolitan transit agency in eastern Massachusetts in the late 1980s, used to have a brown-bag lunch with a group of employees every Friday noon. He brought his lunch, and so did they. These were rank-and-file employees, not top managers. He wanted to talk to the folks who operated and maintained the equipment. He used to remark how different the information he heard from the bus drivers and mechanics was from what he heard from the managers. Those brown-bag lunches were a great morale-builder as well. The top guy really seemed to be interested in what his employees had to say and their suggestions for improving the system.

Federico Peña did the same thing, even though he was responsible for the U.S. Department of Transportation, with its many thousands of employees, during the Clinton administration. "Once a month," said Peña, "I would have a lottery lunch. Any person in the Department of Transportation could submit their name in a basket for this lunch. It was my way of reaching out. For the first time, people started talking to the secretary. I was on the seventh floor and insulated. People would see me and say, 'We've never met a secretary before.'

"We had a lottery where twenty people were chosen to have lunch with me. They would come in and have their little brown bags. I would have a brown sack myself. Anybody could be in the lottery. We'd close the doors. We'd have one staff person in the room, and then I would say to them, 'You can ask me any question you want. Nothing you say will be used against you. So if you have criticism of something or somebody, you can tell me. If you have an idea or something you'd like to try, tell me. Any questions you want to ask."

"I learned a lot," Peña emphasized. "Questions covered almost everything. Some would focus on specific issues like pay raises or a grievance or a complaint that someone hadn't heard from their supervisor in three months. And then someone would ask, 'The president said last week that we are going to do this and do that. Were you in that cabinet meeting and what was the thinking there?' Some questions were very sophisticated. The range of questions was from top to bottom. Even someone would ask, 'How about your family? How are your kids doing?' I would answer the question. There were no rules. Not one."

A question period like this raises a third important point about walking around, and that is the importance of responding. If a leader-manager does purposeful walking around and listening on an ongoing basis, he had better act in response to what he hears. If his employees tell him things that make sense or need doing, and he does nothing about them, then the whole thing is a waste of time—and his people will know it.

A leader-manager is best advised to do his walking around and listening with small groups and plenty of time. Large staff meetings rarely produce anything useful. People are intimidated and will not tell the boss what they really think. Anybody who has run meetings with large groups knows that invariably, after the meeting is over, somebody will come up to the boss and say, "I didn't want to say this publicly at the meeting, but . . ."

Glynn and Peña had the right idea. Do a brown bagger with a relatively small number of people on a regular basis. Do it in a relaxed setting, preferably on the job site so that people can point out specifically what they are talking about. Take a good hour-and-a-half or two to establish good rapport and have a relaxed conversation that is real and candid. Ask a lot of questions. Listen carefully, and then act on what you hear. You will be amazed at the result, both in improved agency operations and in how your employees feel about their job—and about you.

Mick Trainor understood this almost instinctively when he left the military and became a military reporter for the *New York Times*. He knew from his experience in the Marines that informal settings are often the best places to learn about what is really happening, even though we often start with the more formal venues. Trainor asked: "Where did I get my information when reporting on third-world conflicts? Upon arrival, I would go to see our ambassador, counselor, station chief, and/or military attaché. It was largely a courtesy call, as I never learned anything of real importance from official sources. I had to talk to other people in order to see what was going on," Trainor emphasized. "If there was one, I would go to the American Chamber of Commerce. Business interests were important sources of information. In national capitals, the embassies have Marines assigned for internal security. Off duty, they live in a 'Marine House' where every Friday night, historically around the world, they host a happy hour. All the secretaries, drivers, coffee-makers, and others associated with the embassy come for drinks and hors d'oeuvres." These people became a key source of information for Trainor.

Learning in a more formal setting also is important. Experience is certainly a great teacher, but leader-managers can also develop their skills in the classroom. Mary Peters advocated for a learning approach that combined both— classroom learning that was immediately tested through experience. "When we first came back to Arizona [from Indiana]," Peters noted, "I started taking courses when our youngest went to first grade. I took one or two courses at night school to work towards finishing my degree. I started at a community college but ultimately finished up at the University of Phoenix. I am a fan of their learning style. It would have been easier to go to school when I was younger, but I didn't do it that way.

"The University of Phoenix was a school for working adults. What we learned could be applied to the work that we were doing. I found that fascinating. I did a thesis, for example, on privatization of government services at a time when we were trying to do that at my job. I was able to take what I was learning and apply it. The same is true of management courses. My degree is in organizational management, so I took a number of courses in that area. Book learning helped, but the fact that I could take it and almost immediately apply it was very important. I could say, 'This works, and that doesn't.' The real-world experience was so important."

We tend to think of learning as something we do as individuals—by walking around, listening to colleagues, and attending classes—but as a leader-manager, you must also help others to learn if you hope to be successful. Fostering collaboration and support—the topic of the next chapter—is best achieved when your collaborators and supporters share a common knowledge base.

Kim Belshé took this lesson to heart when she began preparing her agency to tackle health-care reform. As she tells the story, "In the summer of 2006, one of my recommendations to colleagues in the governor's office was that if we are serious about a comprehensive universal health proposal—for the governor to announce in January of 2007—we need to build our internal capacity. Already, we had spent quite a bit of time from a policy perspective developing 'Health Care 101' briefings for the governor and his senior staff. This really began back in 2005. We looked at the demographics of California's uninsured, the fundamentals of health care financing delivery, different coverage plans, and other issues."

"One of my recommendations to the chief of staff and the cabinet secretary," Belshé highlighted, "was that all of us—the governor, senior staff, and those in the agency—share a common foundation in terms of information. Recall that Governor Schwarzenegger came to this job with an unusual background. To his credit, he came to office wanting to take on really big, complicated, and difficult issues. He was prepared to lead the charge. I thought it would be helpful to get everyone on the same knowledge base. Our agency organized a series of briefings. The governor was very patient. It was already clear in some respects what he wanted to do, but he also recognized that having a solid foundation of information and policy analysis would be helpful."

Leader-managers also need to be skilled in the use of data. They use data to make decisions and, equally important, their organizations typically rely upon the effective development and management of data. Jean Toal saw data management as one of her most important initiatives as chief justice. "I realized when I became chief justice that we were in a bad turn in our economy, as were most of the states, and we had a crushing backlog of cases. It was very unlikely that we would get new money from the state. In fact, I thought our budget might be cut. I was very unlikely to get new judges or new bricks and mortar. So how could I devise a business process that would bring more efficiency out of the system? What could I do to reengineer the current system to make it work better?

"Technology became the key. I had been attending technology conventions for a number of years. I needed to figure out some way to automate, standardize, and connect the mechanics of how we manage courts, their records, their filings, and the backlog of cases. We needed a better way to move cases through the system. We needed a process instead of this big slop of cases in which assignment was often done by who was screaming the loudest. There wasn't a process for how you push cases through. There weren't deadlines or things that had to happen to get them to move through the system."

"To address problems like this in general," Toal noted, "you need two things to happen. First you need to have a management idea about what kind of process would be a more effective way to manage your system. Second, you need some technique for making that happen. For me, that was using technology. So I had to develop a business process and an underlying methodology."

Tom Payzant provides another example in which the knowledge and management of data are particularly important. As a school superintendent, Payzant had been a strong advocate of data-based decision-making. As he noted in an interview for *Phi Delta Kappan:* "A data-based decision maker is one who uses systematically collected and reported information—information that meets the tests of validity, reliability, and verifiability—as the major factor in choosing among alternatives." This does not mean that intuition, values, politics, and experience are not important, but Payzant argues that data should be used "to test—to check and balance—those other frames of reference that we used for decision making, so that the result is a high quality decision" (Duckett 1985, 437).

Effectively using data is not a simple task. A leader-manager must understand not only the data being discussed—the underlying statistical technique, for example—but also the subtleties of how the data were collected and interpreted. "Data," Payzant says, "are neither collected nor used in a vacuum; they are rarely value-free. The interpretation of data is usually subject to the value system of the decision maker. This implies interplay between the data and the values of the data collectors and of the decision makers who use the data. Data can influence the shaping of values, and values can determine the way data are collected and interpreted. Decision makers must be vigilant in knowing the difference" (Duckett 1985, 437).

5

Fostering Collaboration and Support

In walking around, listening, and learning, leader-managers are reaching out and connecting to others inside and outside the organization. This is an important step in what is a central practice for effective leader-managers: fostering collaboration and support for the organization and its initiatives. Leader-managers do not act alone. They understand the value of collaboration and coalition-building.

Leader-managers must master the ability to reach out to a wide range of people and organizations and bring them into the process of policy-making and implementation from the very beginning. They do this not simply because it is courteous. They do it because they have genuine respect for the people and organizations that care deeply about what they are doing. They also recognize that those key players often know at least as much as, if not more than, they do about the problems they face and how to deal with them.

Nor do they approach collaboration with a chip on their shoulders or with a sense that certain people or groups will automatically oppose what they are trying to do. In public education, for example, many observers of the educational scene, and most often those with little actual hands-on experience in public education, automatically assume that teachers' unions will oppose efforts to change the system or insist on greater accountability.

Tom Payzant did not make that assumption. He understood that teachers were an important part of his educational constituency. Without their active involvement, participation, and support, not only would many of the things he wanted to do be difficult, but also he might well try to do them in ways that would not work effectively.

How, then, did he begin to build a good, constructive, ongoing relationship with his union? By meeting on a regular basis with his union presidents, often without a prearranged agenda. "I learned in San Diego," he said, "the value of one-on-one meetings with union presidents. I learned that little subtleties can make a difference. You need to pay attention to them. Ultimately, the contract will be settled, and there will be another contract. It's a cycle. It was important to de-personalize the process."

He made sure that he approached his relationship with the union in the same way when he came to Boston. "Ed Doherty [the Boston union president] was a veteran. I met him early in my tenure, and my approach to him, and his approach to me, was that regardless of what was going on, we continued to communicate and work together. We had breakfast on a regular basis. At the breakfasts we didn't have a formal agenda. We talked about the pressures and issues we were facing in our respective roles. We stopped short of trying to cut a deal over breakfast. The conversation was typically more exploratory, as in 'what if' kinds of discussions."

Like Payzant, John Catoe understood how important building good relationships with his union leadership could be. He arrived at the Los Angeles Metropolitan Transit Authority in the number two position just as negotiations for a new contract were about to begin. The system had experienced a tough, disruptive strike the last time around. Catoe was determined that this time negotiations would conclude in a constructive fashion and that there absolutely would be no strike.

He received the authority he needed from his board and then began to work with the union and its leadership. "I told them," he said, "that we're lost. We're too old in comparison with the rest of the country. It shocked them. I gave them all the information we had. I didn't hide anything and took a different approach. I can tell you in the beginning, the transit drivers' president was doing his normal style of shaking his finger and raising his voice. I just sat there and started smiling at him. One time when this happened, he said, 'Why are you smiling like that?' And I said, 'James, because I remember my minister in church. He was just like you. He was good. He would give a sermon with his finger shaking. Next thing you know, the collection plate came out. I've worked with you before.' He never raised his finger at me again. We ate together, and we started to talk about our families together. We got to know each other.

"But the key was I told him they were getting a wage increase. It has to be within the national average . . . but you've got to understand where we are as an organization. From a productivity standpoint, I need your help. It worked. We'd never walk out of negotiations. We had someone with us who facilitated and gave us both feedback. She had a union background, so the union trusted her. It worked."

Of course, unions are not the only important constituency to which leader-managers pay attention. In fact, one of the reasons leading and managing effectively in the public sector are so hard is that you face an often bewildering array of people and organizations, all of which have a strong interest in what you are doing and are determined to play a role in what you do. As Gordon Chase and Betsy Reveal note, "the public manager's world is made up of bureaucrats, citizens, and politicians; and in order to get anything done, the public manager must be adept at dealing with all three" (1983, 93).

An effective leader-manager understands this and begins to reach out to all of the key players and constituencies from the beginning. She makes a list of every single key player and constituency that has a real interest in what she does and how she does it. This list includes elected chief executives, legislators, and agency officials both at her level of government and in the other layers of the federal system as well as organized advocacy groups.

Depending on the problem faced, the list may be fairly short. On the other hand, it is often long. With health care, for example, it can involve literally hundreds of key actors and constituencies. On an issue as contentious as health care, a leader-manager may not achieve full consensus; but bringing key players together and involving them genuinely and actively in the process can pay enormous dividends. In fact, if a leader-manager does not understand how to do this, her efforts will be doomed to failure before she even begins.

Kim Belshé understood this as she and Governor Arnold Schwarzenegger attempted to do something that had never been done before in California: win public and legislative support for a plan to provide health insurance for virtually every resident of the state. As Belshé noted: "I knew that if we wanted to do the political work, we needed to have the resources and the assets to make it happen. We hired someone who could focus on external relations and engaging people directly. All of us were involved, but this really was his singular goal. The end point was a very significant coalition of support behind comprehensive health-care reform.

"It involved many business leaders and a number of the large chambers of commerce from around the state actually agreeing that employers should be required to contribute financially to health care. Our coalition involved every health insurer, except one. They agreed that they needed to offer health care to everyone, regardless of pre-existing conditions and that they would support a cap on administrative costs and profit. The coalition included many labor unions, consumer groups, business leaders, and medical providers. The hospital association was supportive of taxing itself to draw additional federal funds and increase coverage."

Of course, Belshé had an important ally, and she used him effectively. "The governor was a critical piece of coalition building. He invested a significant amount of his time in the process. He was personally invested. We would invite people to come in and meet with the governor, bringing all the stakeholder groups involved, including consumer advocate groups and leaders in the business community. The governor was constantly involved, which was really critical to keeping people at the table. When you have the governor of the state of California, or any state, look you in the eye and say, 'Your input is important, your participation is critical; we're going to get there, notwithstanding all the naysayers and things you're hearing from the critics about why reform can't possibly happen,' it keeps people at the table. It keeps people engaged. If the governor calls, they will come."

Jean Toal understood the importance of building coalitions, even within the somewhat constrained environment in which a state supreme court chief justice operates. Undoubtedly, her experience as one of South Carolina's most respected legislators contributed to this understanding. "I was quite young," Toal commented, "when I was elected to the legislature, and I was one of a small number of women. I came to the General Assembly in 1975 after the November 1974 elections with a group of fifty-two new people. I brought the group together and formed a freshman caucus. We were all very different, and we had a lot of diversity among us, but we were united in the desire to be effective and to have a new voice heard. We wanted a new way of doing things and not just the 'good old boy' system."

"In the freshman caucus," Toal noted, "there were Republicans, Democrats, small county people, big county people, and others. We were all over the place. We would never agree on issues. We'd end up divided and conquered by others before we even started. We needed something we could be together on. We found it in the question 'How can this institution run better?'"

She brought that collaborative style to her role as the state's chief justice and chief court administrator, particularly as she introduced major new information technology into the South Carolina court system to cope with a major backlog of cases. "To make this happen," Toal noted, "I brought together a broad group of people who worked out in the field in the court system. They included clerks of court, magistrate judges, lawyers, and other court personnel. These weren't people with the titles, but the people who were out there every day trying to run the court system, particularly in the small rural counties. Some of the larger counties had their systems, but the small rural counties really had very little. I got them together, and we began to talk about what was needed to make them more effective in doing their jobs.

"They were a fairly representative group, racially and geographically. I scrounged a little bit of money to hire a consulting firm to give us some advice, and we developed an Internet-based system to manage court records. Everybody uses the Internet now. Everybody can learn the keyboard as it's taught now. Many of these people are women, working in back rooms. They are in control with these kinds of tools. There are some African-American guys that never had much fun with education, but this has made them successful. They love it. From a leadership standpoint, it makes a lot of sense to involve the people who use it and who are served by it."

Justice Toal does not ignore governors and legislators either. She is a great believer in meeting informally with the governor and key legislators on important justice and court-related issues. As Toal highlighted: "The speaker of the house, the president pro tempore of the senate, the chairs of the two judiciary committees and the finance committees, I make it my business to keep in touch with all these folks. Over time, they've seen the value of keeping in touch with me." She meets with the governor "probably every other week" and with legislative leaders regularly. As Toal concluded: "It takes time to build these relationships. You build trust that way."

To help build those relationships, she also does something very few other chief justices traditionally do. She gives an annual talk to the legislature. "As a member of the General Assembly," Toal noted, "I sponsored the legislation to make that happen. At the time, we had a very poisonous relationship between the legislature and the court. For several years, it was a very bitter relationship that was very destructive and kept us from being able to move the state forward. I sponsored a piece of legislation that invited the chief justice to give a state of the judiciary speech every year to the General Assembly. It's very important to have this kind of public coming together."

In addition, Toal includes the organized bar in her efforts to build collaboration throughout the legal and judicial system. "The organized bar was off by itself when I joined the court, but they are very involved with the court now and vice versa. I think that we've developed a relationship that doesn't typically exist in other states."

Mary Peters discovered the importance of collaboration and coalition-building when she was a contract officer in the Arizona Department of Transportation. Her director decided that turning one of their freeways into a toll road might well be a solution to serious funding problems. Unfortunately, Peters and two of her colleagues were asked to do this without any effort to reach out to key players and constituencies, and the proposal bombed.

She never forgot that lesson. When she became director, she understood that she and Governor Hull would never get a freeway system built if they didn't "rethink and reprioritize it." As Peters noted: "If we developed a plan in the back halls of the agency and dropped it on people—no matter how good the plan was—everybody would find something wrong with it. Instead, build-

43

ing a coalition is what makes it effective. How do you build a coalition? To start, you communicate. Make sure we all want the same thing, because too often people don't want the same thing. You have to coordinate with some people, make sure they're on board with it. You have to define what's really important. We used the phrase, 'what's going home for us.' What at the end of the day has to be in this bill to make it work for you?"

To build support for this project, she met weekly with a working group that involved important legislators, including the speaker and the president of the senate, and a number of business leaders along with key legislative staffers. "We developed the plans going into the fall, wrote the legislation in November, dropped it in the legislative hopper in December, released it in January, and in May it was law. We really didn't get the press involved until the package went to the legislature. Then they became very curious, and here's where the coalition-building was so important. They went around with a microphone and notepad and asked people, 'What do you think of this?' Because we had done the work to build the coalition, the opinion leaders that they talked to were supportive."

For many leader-managers, successful collaborations happen only after a series of failures and tough lessons. Michael Dukakis, despite eight years of legislative experience, did not really understand the dynamic of coalition-building in his first term as governor, especially when it came to working with his former colleagues in the Massachusetts legislature. He had been a rebel and a reformer in his legislative days. Providing leadership as governor required a very different and a much more collaborative approach in his dealings with the legislature. It took a painful defeat in 1978 and a lot of thinking about those relationships while he was out of office to help him understand that legislators can and must be involved in a chief executive's policy decisions from the beginning, not after he and his staff on their own have decided what they want to do. These relationships were important in supporting immediate goals, or they would become "money in the bank" as support for future activities. Former Florida governor and U.S. senator Bob Graham had a particularly apt way of describing that process. "You need to sell stock in your ideas so that members of the legislature feel that this is as much their program as it is the governor's program."

Fostering collaboration is important at every level of an organization, in the nonprofit sector as well as government. John Portz, as a newly hired director of a university undergraduate honors program, found his existing contacts and relationships inadequate for the job. As a member of the faculty, he had limited contacts with administrators and other faculty, particularly in the other colleges of the university. Yet the honors program depended upon support from administrators, faculty, staff, and students in all parts of the university.

As the new director, one of his first actions was to meet with key administrators in each of the university's six colleges. In most instances this was the associate dean responsible for undergraduate education. The primary purpose was to begin developing relationships with these individuals. Each administrator had a different history with the honors program, some more positive than others, and each had a particular perspective on the best future path for the program. These first meetings focused on introductions and laying the groundwork for a professional relationship. This was not the time to raise controversial issues, but rather to understand the administrators' perspectives as they related to the honors program. These meetings were important first steps in building relationships with individuals who would play a key role in the future success of the program.

Even leader-managers who develop the critically important ability to bring people together and build coalitions will not always succeed, however. Kim Belshé and her governor were unable to get a sweeping and creative health reform plan through the California legislature, in part because getting that kind of legislation passed requires a two-thirds vote in California, and the governor simply could not get the votes he needed to get the bill approved. But it was not for lack of outreach and the building of a powerful coalition that included business, labor, health-care providers, and health insurers. In the end, ideology on both the right and the left in the legislature thwarted their work. But they have laid a strong foundation for future efforts—something that would be inconceivable without the kind of collaboration and support that they developed across a broad spectrum of the California community.

As one can see from the work of some of our leader-managers, there is no single way to encourage the kind of collaboration that is so essential to effective public leadership and management. All of our leader-managers do it in ways that make sense to them and fit the institutional framework in which they work. In most cases, creating a working group of key leaders and representatives of organizations chaired either by the leader-manager or staff that reports directly to her is an essential first step. Every effort should be made to identify each of them and get them to the table, no matter what their apparent view of the issue and its potential solution.

Nor does it matter that they have publicly differed on the subject. When Kim Belshé first involved chambers of commerce in California in the effort to produce a health reform plan, it was the first time many of those organizations had ever endorsed the notion that all employers had an obligation to contribute to the system. In the end, however, it was not surprising that they did so. Most of their members provided health insurance for their employees and discovered in the course of their deliberations that they were paying what the governor correctly called a hidden tax of some $1,500 per premium to pay for free care for employees whose employers were either unable or unwilling to insure them and their families.

Working hard to involve key legislators and constituencies in the process is particularly important during economic recessions. Federico Peña points out that "being mayor is not much fun when you are in a major recession. There's nothing worse for a leader . . . than a recession. It is painful because people are hurting. There's a lot of pressure. I was working seven days a week. I was out every night speaking to practically any group who wanted to hear from me. These were long hours requiring difficult, painful decisions."

It is precisely in these kinds of situations, however, that collaboration and consensus-building are most important. Yes, people are angry, but if the leader-manager brings them together and lays out in detail exactly what the fiscal problems are and what the budget-cutting target is, people will work together to try to make the right decisions. Often, they know more than the budget director does about where the waste is and where more efficient and productive operations can produce savings. Nothing is worse in these circumstances than mindless across-the-board cuts that fail to include the active involvement of concerned legislators, constituencies, and the agency's own rank-and-file employees.

Anyone who has been involved in this process can tell you that remarkable things happen if the leader-manager and her staff have the ability and the skill to get the process moving and the participants talking. For one thing, in most cases they will at least agree on what the problem is—and that is a critical first step on the way to a solution. Second, as they begin to know and respect each other, they come to understand that most, if not all, of the people around the table share the same common values. Who, after all, in California or the nation, for that matter, thinks it is a good thing that we have 47 million Americans, most of them working or members of working families, without a dime of health insurance? Who is happy about the fact that when they show up in the emergency room because they do not have and cannot afford a primary doctor, we are all paying for their medical care either as premium payers or taxpayers?

Often, a kind of chemistry develops in which people who were taking shots at each other through the media or in public forums begin to understand that they have a common interest in solving the challenge they face. As the process unfolds, they learn more about ideas that they may be considering for the first time as a result of the ongoing meetings and deliberations of the working group. The important point to bear in mind, however, is that without the initiative of the leader-manager there would be no working group and no chemistry but rather the kind of standoff that so often frustrates Americans as they watch their governments struggle to find solutions to the serious problems they face.

If the process goes well and consensus is reached, the stage is set to win legislative approval, if required, and to create and implement programs that can achieve the group's goals. Quite obviously, the leader-manager has to assume political leadership as the process goes forward, but she is now doing it with an impressive coalition behind her that has participated fully in developing those recommendations and is thus committed to seeing them through. And when the press comes calling, as they did when Mary Peters had put her freeway legislation together, they find an impressive cadre of people and organizations who have joined together in support of recommendations that are, in a very real sense, theirs.

Developing the ability to bring people together in a collaborative and constructive way is not genetic. Most of us have to learn it the hard way, but there is no reason for leader-managers to make the same mistakes over and over again, as they often do when they are proposing new policy initiatives. Hiring a consultant or surrounding themselves with bright young graduates of public-policy schools may at times be helpful. However, they are no substitute for the open and collaborative process that is an absolutely essential part of getting things done in the public sector.

Building Effective Organizations

Leader-managers work within and across organizations to achieve their goals. Our focus in the last chapter on collaboration highlighted the challenges of working with people to build a common agenda and implement policies and programs. Our interest in this chapter is the organizational side of the equation. Leader-managers must learn to successfully navigate the structure of authority, power, and influence that exists within and between organizations.

An important starting point is the power and authority that come with a leader-manager's organizational position. As Jean Toal noted: "South Carolina has what is known as a 'strong' chief justice. I have a lot of administrative authority. Some chief justices in other states are much weaker in authority. While they are head of their court and have some central administrative responsibility, much of the administration is in the hands of local, county, or regional governments. These chief justices are neither the boss of it nor in control of it. I, on the other hand, have authority over the entire statewide judicial system, and I have the responsibility of asking for money to fund a good deal of what's done. There is some county funding for some of the projects, but my budget includes a lot of what's needed to function. The culture and expectation is to look to the chief justice for advice as to how the rest of the system should operate."

This organizational authority is important. It provides Toal with the institutional base from which she can push for change in the South Carolina court system. It gives her key policy and management tools, like control of the budget, that help her to achieve her goals. To be sure, this authority, as well as the ability to organize or reorganize a system or agency, is not a guarantee of success, but it does provide a platform for action. Toal used this position to launch a major technology overhaul of the court system, among other initiatives.

In the education world, Thomas Payzant was similarly thankful for legislative changes that gave him authority over his school principals. As Payzant commented in his interview: "One of the best things that ever happened in the 1993 [Massachusetts] state reform law was when superintendents were given control over personnel, and principals were taken out of collective bargaining. If principals had stayed in collective bargaining here, I would not have been able to lead the district with a major commitment to develop and appoint principals who could lead instrumental improvement and raise achievement."

For both Toal and Payzant—and any leader-manager—the authority and resources that come with a particular organizational position are important. Chief Justice Toal used her position to drive change in the court system; Superintendent Payzant's authority over school principals was a critical piece in his reform effort. Whether as secretary or director at the top of an organization or a bureau or section chief at the lower levels, the authority and resources of a leader-manager's organizational position provide key tools in addressing the challenges that lie ahead.

Using your position is an important starting point in developing effective organizations, but there are many more challenges. One of the most important is designing an appropriate system of reporting levels within the unit. For Mary Peters, her major goal in designing these levels was improving communication among all participants. As she noted in a radio interview: "I was fortunate in that I inherited an organization [Federal Highway Administration] that had gone through a rather substantial reorganization in 1998 and eliminated a number of layers. What we want to do is have no more than two levels between ourselves and our field offices so that ultimately, we are communicating well and carrying out a clear sense of strategic direction. So in my office, myself as administrator, a deputy administrator and executive director, communicate with directors of field services, who then work with our field offices. So we have those few layers. I think that helps us tremendously in communicating well and being consistent across the organization" (Center for the Business of Government 2002, 4).

Peters was grappling with the classic "org chart" that characterizes most public agencies. In a hierarchical fashion, front-line employees work for supervisors, who in turn report to mid-level managers, who report to other supervisors or managers higher up the chain of command. In graphic form, the boxes of an org chart represent positions or units connected to other boxes by lines, signifying reporting and supervisory relationships.

The test for a leader-manager is figuring out how to draw these lines and establish reporting relationships that will most effectively achieve the goals of the organization.

Tom Payzant faced this very test when he was hired as superintendent of the Boston Public Schools. As he recalled: "The organization I inherited in 1995 had several layers of administration between the superintendent and the schools. The transition team [a group of educational leaders he had asked to review the school system] made clear to me that the principals—who reported to assistant superintendents for elementary, middle, and high schools—felt disconnected from the superintendent. The assistant superintendents reported to a deputy superintendent, who was one of several members of a senior leadership group that reported to the superintendent. My reorganization plan eliminated the level offices (elementary, middle, and high) and had the principals report directly to the superintendent. This was an important symbolic step based on my belief that principals are one of the most important factors in our systemic plan to improve schools and raise student achievement" (Payzant and Horan 2007, 253).

This was an unusual move. Payzant now had all 125 principals reporting to him. He added his deputy superintendent to the mix to assist with this supervisory responsibility, but he recognized that such an arrangement was not sustainable for the long term. One, and even two, individuals could not effectively supervise and evaluate 125 people while still being responsible for a host of other activities within the system. Still, redesigning the organization in this manner was, even if temporarily, an important way to highlight the key role principals play in a school system. As Payzant emphasized in our interview, "the most important decision in designing a [school district's] organization is to determine who will be responsible for selecting, supervising, and evaluating the principals." Payzant was using this organizational strategy to send a clear message to principals and the broader school community that principals are leaders in school reform.

Within a couple of years, Payzant made another organizational design change to further strengthen the role of principals and enhance leadership development within the organization. He developed a "cluster system" in which schools were grouped into ten geographic clusters. Each cluster was composed of elementary, middle, and high schools that were in proximity to one another. As Payzant described it: "Clusters were geographic, each with about twelve schools. The cluster leader, who was a principal at one of the twelve schools, was on my leadership team. Cluster leaders did not supervise their colleagues, but acted as conveners. I assigned the best principals to be cluster leaders. They were paid $1,000 a month to be conveners and sounding boards. Those ten cluster leaders were part of my senior leadership group;

they were involved in decision-making. We met every two weeks for two hours. I was constantly sending the message that they were important, and I wanted to know what was going on out in the schools and seek their guidance on district policy and budget issues."

It is interesting to note that Payzant's cluster approach encouraged and actually formalized a nonhierarchical relationship among school principals. The twelve principals in one cluster developed a mutual support system in which collaboration and sharing among peers was the explicit goal. The principals shared best practices and focused on various ways to improve their respective schools. The cluster leader did not supervise or otherwise assume authority over the other principals in the cluster. This organizational design, then, was meant to foster learning among peers rather than change reporting relationships and lines of authority.

If Tom Payzant saw clusters as a way to improve the work of principals within the school system, Michael Dukakis launched a new organization and reconnected existing organizations to better address a pressing external need. In his first term as governor, Massachusetts faced serious economic challenges. Massachusetts, and New England in general, were being called "the new Appalachia." Massachusetts had the second highest unemployment rate in the nation—over 12 percent at its peak—and unemployment in many of its older industrial communities exceeded 20 percent. Focusing on those industrial communities was one of his most important goals. This required effective communication and coalition-building with local and state officials (a topic of the previous chapter), but it also required a redesign in the organization of state government.

The State Office of Planning and Development (SOPD) and the "development cabinet" were the response. No state government in the country had tried to mount a sweeping urban development effort prior to that time. Dukakis knew what he wanted to achieve, but there was no handy menu sitting on a shelf that told him how to do it. He needed a different way of organizing the state's effort to make this work. In 1975, he hired Frank Keefe to take the lead in this effort as the first director of the new State Office of Planning and Development. From that organizational base, Keefe reached out to key players and worked closely with legislators and local officials along with business and labor.

For Dukakis, a new state unit was needed to focus the resources and expertise of state government and to provide a venue for local officials to connect with the state. Even with this new office, coordination among existing agencies was needed, so they took another step. A "development cabinet" began meeting regularly. This included five key cabinet secretaries who were most deeply involved in the economic and community development process and also the lieutenant-governor, who was in charge of federal-state relations. Keefe chaired those meetings, but it was important to have each of the secretaries at the table. This was not a top-down process, however; if it had been, it would have failed. Virtually every community in the state was deeply involved, and it was out of that process that the first detailed state urban policy emerged and was aggressively implemented.

Whereas Dukakis created a new organization and reconnected several existing ones, another common organizational strategy is to revive and re-constitute an existing part of an organization to help it better achieve specific goals. John Portz, in his role as university honors program director, did just that with a long-standing faculty advisory committee for the program. Faced with a university directive to expand the honors curriculum and also transition from a quarter-based to a semester-based system, Portz looked to an existing advisory committee for help. He added key administrators to the committee, such as associate deans from several colleges who were responsible for un-dergraduate curriculum, and ensured that each college in the university was represented by a member of the faculty. He chaired the committee, which allowed him to set the agenda and pace for the group. He purposely included at least a few individuals on the committee who had been critical of some aspects of the program in the past. He wanted those people to be constructive inside the organization rather than outside critics.

This reconstituted committee played a key role in shaping the new honors program. The committee did a self-assessment of strengths and weaknesses of the current program and reviewed initiatives and other best practices at honors programs in other universities. A mission statement for the program was refined and key goals and action strategies were identified, including the introduction of new honors seminars.

There are many ways to redraw the lines of an org chart, and there are many different purposes in doing so. Mary Peters provides one example in her focus on reducing the number of levels in the organization with a goal of improved communication. Tom Payzant's clusters offer a different example in which more informal relationships are fostered to improve learning among peers. Sometimes the explicit intent is to redraw lines to alter the chain of command and shift organizational responsibilities among employees. In other cases, as with Dukakis's development cabinet and Payzant's clusters, the strategy is less about major changes in the formal hierarchy and more about simply improving communication and coordination through more interaction among key players.

This later example brings to mind the rising importance of networks as an organizational strategy. Networks typically refer to a collection of individuals and/or organizations that work together to achieve certain goals, but without the usual lines of authority that are found in a hierarchy. Networks are part of a "shared-power world" (Crosby and Bryson 2005) in which discussions and negotiations among network members, like the secretaries of the development cabinet, yield a result to which all have contributed. In this environment, leader-managers do not command specific actions; rather, they negotiate with others to achieve common goals.

Beyond redrawing the lines of authority in an organization, leader-managers also need to understand the rules and culture that develop in different organizations. From legislatures to executive bureaucracies to courts to universities to the military, organizations develop different rules, norms, and practices about how people interact. Legislative bodies, for example, are steeped in rules and norms around seniority, partisanship, and reciprocity. The military, on the other hand, has a culture in which rank and authority are particularly prominent. Leader-managers may have an opportunity to shift or tweak rules and culture to their own liking, but in most cases, their approach is to learn how to navigate this environment to achieve their own goals.

Kim Belshé described two organizational rules that have a significant impact on the ability of leader-managers in California to craft compromises involving elected officials. One rule involves voting requirements for the state legislature, and the other concerns party primaries. "What's unique, or semi-unique to California," Belshé explained, "is that we are one of only three states that require a two-thirds vote to pass the budget. Also, we are one of only a handful of states that require a two-thirds vote to raise a tax. In the absence of divided government, this may be a good idea. But it is a reality that gives significant authority to the minority, which in California's case is typically Republicans. It makes it very difficult for the legislature to pass a budget or raise a tax."

Another rule that shapes political organizations and impacts the coalition-building process is the closed nature of party primaries. In California, as in some other states, state primary elections are open only to those who have registered in that party. For example, to vote in the Democratic primary, a person must be registered as a Democrat. "As a result," Belshé concluded, "you have Democrats competing to be the most Democratic, and you have Republicans competing to be the most Republican. Each is appealing to their voter base that will come out in the primary election. We do not have a middle in our capital—we really don't. We have very conservative Republicans and very liberal or progressive Democrats."

The result is that California politics has become polarized, without a political middle. Leader-managers seeking to move an agenda forward face a formidable task. For Belshé, these rules contributed to the downfall of a major health-care reform initiative. The issue became polarized and failed to garner sufficient support to move it forward in the legislature. The bottom line: organizational rules can create significant hurdles for leader-managers.

Jean Toal provided another example in which organizational rules, those of the legislature in this case, played an important part. As noted in Chapter 5, when Toal was first elected to the South Carolina General Assembly she brought together the fifty-two new representatives into the freshman caucus. Not only was this an example of building collaboration and support, it also involved recrafting an existing organization. As she remembers the experience, "My thought was to bring these people together so we could learn the rules and be effective. We really did reform the system rather substantially, and I'm proud of my leadership role in that. We learned the rules and became empowered to be very effective on the House floor. Sometimes we could figure out ways to move things forward that even surprised the older members. For example, we changed the filibuster rule, which so inhibited the free discussion of a lot of different ideas. Just by our excitement about issues, we promoted more debate on the House floor and more openness to discussion."

Mick Trainor's career crossed from the military arena to a university, two quite different organizational environments. They required different approaches. "You can be far more direct within the military about what you want done. It's still leadership, but it's a little more direct. In civilian life, when I was at the university, there was no real hierarchy. It's a somewhat chaotic organization. Persuasion and example are far more important in the academic world than when I was in the military side of the house. So in dealing with a recalcitrant professor whom you want to teach a certain element in one of your programs, and he is disinclined to do it, you have to bring in far more persuasion instead of simply saying, 'I want you to do this.' When you're dealing with people who are co-equals, persuasion is very important, and you have to develop techniques that don't depend upon the stars on your shoulder."

Tom Payzant, upon his arrival in Washington, DC, as an assistant secretary in the U.S. Department of Education, faced a new culture in the nation's capital. In particular, working with Congress became an essential task. As he described it: "I was in Washington at a very interesting time. I had the opportunity to work on Goals 2000, a major piece of legislation. I learned a lot that later benefited my work in Boston. It was a different environment. When the White House called, or when Secretary of Education Richard Riley called, I responded immediately. I had never left so many people in the waiting room as I did in Washington. I would go to so many events—endless events—but I got used to that whole culture.

"This was new to me. I had worked with state legislatures in the past, but this was different. Some questioned whether I could get the job done; they would say, 'He doesn't know how to work inside the Beltway.' I did a lot of testifying on Capitol Hill. I had been working with school boards and state legislatures for a long time. I thought, 'What's so different about this big legislature on the hill?' I actually did fine. I was honest with them. If I didn't know something, I would say, 'You'll have the information tomorrow.' And I wouldn't give them convoluted, long answers to their questions. In addition, I had a good relationship with the staffers. There were not many [education] practitioners in congressional leadership positions; members of Congress responded positively to candid answers about how policy proposals would affect educators and students in school districts and schools."

Federico Peña faced the same problem with the Federal Aviation Administration (FAA) when, after eight years as Denver's mayor, he became Secretary of Transportation in a new Clinton administration. "In the FAA, you would bring in your own administrator, [but] I found that changing the culture . . . was very challenging. It took a long time, and I am not sure that we were ever fully successful. The problem was that the FAA had a reputation of having what was called a 'tombstone mentality' in which they would wait until after an accident had happened before they would finally change safety standards.

"The National Transportation Safety Board was always pressuring the FAA, saying 'Why haven't you passed this rule?' The FAA would say, 'Well, we've only had two accidents, and it's going to cost industry too much. There's no sense in doing it.' I was of the other view. I was always pushing the FAA, saying, 'Let's move forward; let's require these safety rules.' The problem was that in the recession of the early '90s the airlines had lost $12 billion. It was challenging for the FAA as an institution to require bankrupt airlines to make hundred-million-dollar investments for safety equipment."

In his transition from the legislature to the governor's office, Michael Dukakis crossed the boundaries between two very different organizational cultures. As he admits, he had a lot to learn. As an organization, the legislature was very much controlled by the Senate president and House speaker. By and large, Dukakis had been an outsider to that leadership structure in the legislature, a "reformer" who worked against the dominant rules and culture of the organization, but he was aware of how the leadership controlled the agenda. When he became governor, the world changed dramatically. He was now at the top of an organization—the executive branch and governor's office—in which bureaucratic expertise was important, but was mixed with political realities.

As governor, Dukakis was "learning the ropes" of operating in a different organizational setting. Like most leader-managers, he was developing the knowledge and skills to build an effective organization. As we have seen, the authority and resources that come with a particular organizational position are an important part of the story. Jean Toal and most of our other interviewees were thankful for the authority they received by virtue of their position. Perhaps the most difficult task is coming up with the organizational design—redrawing the org chart—that will best achieve the goals of the organization. There is no magic formula. Sometimes more centralized control is needed, but for other purposes, decentralization of authority and action to the field offices is most important. In short, there are a variety of creative ways to align organizational structure and purpose. Finally, leader-managers need to be aware of the rules and culture that shape an organization. They must develop the skills to navigate this important part of the terrain.

Taking advantage of organizational authority, redesigning organizations, and navigating organizational cultures are important, but as we emphasized in an earlier chapter, a critical piece to the puzzle is identifying the right people to fill the positions in the organization. As any leader-manager knows, an organization chart is only as good as the people who occupy the positions. As Tom Payzant concluded: "In developing an organization, we often start in the pure sense of having the organization the way we would like it, but then there is the reality of who fills the positions on the chart. Sometimes I have had to alter the organizational chart and reporting lines to get the right fit. You can create the most beautiful organizational design, but if you don't have the right people, with the necessary skills in the right places, the organization won't work."

7

Communicating With the Public

Leader-managers communicate in many ways, some of which we have already discussed.

They manage by walking around and engaging in the kind of easy, informal conversation with their employees that not only provides them with valuable information, but also gives them a chance to get to know the people on whom they are relying to implement their agenda.

They cast a wide net and tap into their own networks to identify the best candidates to serve as staff in the organization, and they seek through various means to motivate these employees.

They foster coalitions by reaching out to key players across the political and civic spectrum, bringing them into the policy process in a genuine way and working with them to develop and build political support for policy initiatives.

They build effective organizational structures that bring staff together to foster and support communications within the organization as well as with other organizations.

They are good listeners, and they learn from listening.

Above all, they develop means to communicate effectively with a broad and diverse public. Leader-managers take their relationship with the public seriously; they recognize that it is a very important part of their job; and they approach the public positively with a broad communications strategy that can help them win public support for their programs and engage the public, particularly those whom they seek to help, in constructive and meaningful ways. They recognize that from time to time they will be subject to scrutiny and criticism, but they understand that that is part of their job, and they are ready for it. They understand that managing their public image and public relations is just as important as any other management responsibility they face.

Tom Payzant understood this clearly. "Just as schools need families to be involved in their children's education, the school system needs the ongoing support and investment of the community in order to achieve its educational goals. Therefore, it is essential that citizens, taxpayers, funders, partners, media, elected officials, opinion leaders, and countless others are aware of the state of the city schools, both their progress and their challenges moving forward. To strengthen the lines of communication, in 2005 we launched a multifaceted strategic communications initiative and appointed the district's first chief communications officer to lead the work. The initiative is rooted in the premise that improving communication is not separate from the teaching and learning agenda, but rather, essential to its success. Only when we do a better job of telling our story and identifying our gaps can we foster the confidence and investment needed to achieve our educational goals."

The communications strategy introduced by Payzant is instructive for its approach to the challenges facing public agencies. Titled "Strategic Communications: Engaging the Community in Educational Success," this twenty-one-page document outlined a "multifaceted approach to delivering a positive, proactive, coherent, consistent message about the strengths and challenges of Boston's schools" (Boston Public Schools 2006, 2). The communications strategy sought to increase awareness and positive public perceptions of the schools while also generating more engagement and support among the public, including parents and others in the community. A media strategy was central to this effort, but also the report outlined a role for the Internet, telephone, and general publications. As in the private sector, the schools needed to market and brand their product, while conducting market research to track and assess the public image of the schools.

The media play a key role in any communications strategy. The Boston schools' strategy highlighted the need to build positive relationships with reporters, and it also emphasized the importance of being proactive in getting positive stories into the media. For leader-managers, a sound media strategy is a must. This is particularly true for elected leader-managers and those at the top of the organization. Even for mid- and lower-level managers, who are often subject to organizational rules that limit their authority to interact with the media, understanding and participating in the organization's media strategy is an important part of their role.

John Catoe took his media relations just as seriously as Payzant. In fact, he had no choice. He knew that the Washington Metro was an important part of the community. People in the city identified with the system. As he noted, people often "describe where they are living by the nearest Metro station. Another time, people would say, 'Yes, we took Metro to get here.' When you hear that from the public, you know that they appreciate the system. They see it as their system. We're fortunate to have that level of interest."

That level of interest is reflected in the Metro's press coverage. "The *Washington Post*," Catoe noted, "has a reporter who gives front-page coverage a lot. Her entire job is Metro; that's all she does. So the *Post* plays a role in setting the agenda. The publisher is Donald Graham. His mother was Katherine Graham, who owned the *Post*. My mother worked for her; my mother was the person who made sure the menu was correct in the executive dining room. We talked about that; that's how we opened [one of our early] meetings. It was an emotional experience for both of us. My mother was very close to Katherine Graham. We talked, in front of the others on the executive board about what our mothers would say now. Look where their sons are. We connected emotionally."

However, Catoe would be the first to tell you that even those personal ties with the publisher of the paper of record in the nation's capital would not shield him from unrelenting press scrutiny if he did not meet his goal of turning the Washington Metro into the best transit system in the country. Catoe understood, as Tom Payzant understood, that he had to take his media relations seriously and manage them effectively if he was going to win the public support he needed to make some tough fiscal and management decisions in the months ahead.

Media relations are important to the leader-manager for a whole host of reasons. Perhaps most importantly, as Catoe and Payzant both understand, they help to build public and political support for your agenda. In fact, as John Catoe so perceptively pointed out, the media often set your agenda for you. If you and your agency are subject to a tough, six-part series on what is wrong with a particular aspect of what you are doing, you had better take that series seriously and respond to it. Otherwise, you will face a story a day about why you are not responding, and pretty soon your elected or appointed superiors may decide they want a different leader-manager. Indeed, press scrutiny regarding a tragic accident at the Washington Metro in 2009 and related problems contributed to Catoe's resignation in early 2010.

Good press helps to build credibility with special constituencies and advocacy groups whose support and help you need. Newspaper readership is declining in this country, but many constituencies and key groups still read the papers every day. Further, they increasingly scrutinize everything that comes over the Internet that may affect you or your agency. In fact, these days they write their own copy and post it. Leader-managers ignore those groups and their blogs at their peril.

Good press helps a lot with elected officials and especially the chief executive for whom you work. He usually reads the daily newspapers at about six in the morning. You had better be ready for a phone call when you arrive at the office if the morning news is not good.

Good press affects the share of the budget you are likely to get. Budget directors read the papers, too. If you are getting consistently good press and public exposure, you are likely to be received a lot more favorably at budget-making time by the people that make budget recommendations to the chief.

Good press makes it easier to attract good people to work for you. Also, it builds good morale and real credibility with the people you are depending on to get things done. A story praising the performance of your employees and the work they do does not hurt either. It is a form of employee recognition that can have an enormous effect on the energy and enthusiasm of your agency.

The media help you become a better leader-manager because they are in a very real sense a part of your information system. Leader-managers learn things from taking the press seriously, and while some of those things may not be pleasant, they are an important part of the information flow that can guide your decisions and help set your priorities. John Catoe was reminded of this every day by that full-time Metro reporter who roams the Washington metropolitan area looking for what is going right—and, even more often, what is going wrong—in the national capital's transit system.

Moreover, managing the media effectively can add immeasurably to the kind of "social marketing" that Kim Belshé was trying to do as she began the process of putting together a comprehensive health-care reform plan for California. Of course, it did not hurt that she was working for a governor who had a lot of prior experience with the media. His status as a popular movie actor prior to becoming governor meant he was well known among the media and that he was experienced and comfortable working with reporters and others from the media. "I've had the good fortune," Belshé said, "of working with a governor over the past four years who is extraordinary at attracting media attention. To accommodate the media, we've had to move many of his public speaking events out of the capital building, where governors have historically conducted press events, to major auditoriums. Media coverage of what is going on in Sacramento, historically pretty sparse in the state's major media markets, has jumped dramatically with Arnold Schwarzenegger in the governor's office."

"We work hard," Belshé said, "at engaging key reporters in health and human services. We try to develop relationships that support communication to get the information out in a timely way so we're never accused of hiding the ball. We try to be as transparent as possible. Our health reform team has been very proactive at engaging the media around health reform."

Belshé's media work has not been focused exclusively on her health reform plan, however. Obesity is another Schwarzenegger priority. "We have partnered with non-general fund organizations such as the California Children and Families Commission to invest in obesity prevention and social marketing strategies targeting parents and young children. We've also utilized federal nutrition services block grant funding to develop social marketing strategies that focus on moms as the primary decision-makers in most households. Our anti-tobacco efforts continue to be very effective . . . supported by separate funding from the tobacco tax. Whether free or paid, the media is a key partner in communicating clear and consistent messages around California's health and human services priorities."

In short, the media can be a valuable ally when a leader-manager actively seeks to implement her priorities. That is true when it comes to public health. It is equally true when a state highway department wants to warn people about congestion as a result of major construction projects. It is especially true in times of national disaster. A leader-manager who does not have an excellent press operation is going to have a very hard time dealing with blizzards, hurricanes, and earthquakes if her press operation is not first-rate.

If you want the press to be an ally, it is important to be responsive and focused. John Portz, at a program manager level in a university, interacts with the press largely through phone inquiries from reporters. Based on his perspective and experience, he stresses two key points when working with the press. First, it is important to be timely in responding. Both newspaper reporters and radio and TV newscasters have deadlines that must be met. A response after the deadline does not help anyone. Second, it is crucial to give very focused and to-the-point responses to the questions. Long responses with options of "maybe this" or "maybe that" will not make it into the article. Be on target: What is the key message you want to convey? Be prepared to provide that focused information.

The press is not easy. Reporters are likely to spend a lot more time looking for bad news than good news. For reasons that are hard to understand, they think bad news is more interesting than good news—except when it comes to reporting baseball scores. They have their own mythology. They tend to be cynical. They think that a lot of public officials are either flabby or crooked or both. They believe that exposing the truth will bring about a demand for change.

They often are very thin-skinned. They can dish it out, but they have a hard time taking it. As one prominent columnist said many years ago, "Reporters aren't thin skinned. They have no skin."

There are certain qualities in their work that are very important and that a leader-manager must understand. They have to work fast to meet their editor's deadlines. They try hard to be accurate and are sensitive to charges that they are not. They are very wary of efforts to manipulate them, and they want, understandably, to feel that they are influential. They prefer hard news, human-interest stories, conflict, and tragedy.

Like all elected chief executives, Federico Peña knew that the press would be all over him as he moved into the mayor's office in Denver. Not only would he be the subject of heightened media attention, but appointees to his administration would also face a high degree of media scrutiny, especially if they had never worked in the public sector. However, even though he expected this attention, it caught him by surprise. "When I was in the legislature," Peña said, "the media didn't really follow me because I was the minority leader. It wasn't very intense. I really had a wake-up call when I was mayor. I experienced an avalanche of media attention. I had to watch everything I said and everything I did. This was different from the campaign. This was very intense. Some of it was friendly, but some of it was not.

"At first I was very naive about the media. I had this notion that they would just naturally like me. I was a 'good guy.' Why would anybody not like me? I won the election. I had to learn the hard way. . . . With interviews, I needed to learn how to answer questions, to not deviate and roam, which we're all prone to do. But also, there was the notion of looking at an interview as a chess game. The only way to judge if you were successful was when you made certain points. If you don't say those things, you failed. I'd never heard that before. I had to learn that."

Peña worked with his staff to develop a media strategy that involved more than just playing good defense. Peña and his people understood that, managed properly, the press could help in building support for their key initiatives. As Peña explained it, "my chief of staff and media leader would say, 'Look, this week we really ought to be talking about the environment. So let's do three environment events or announcements.' . . . They'd present the plan. They'd say, 'This month we're going to have to do this, next month we're going to do this, and in six months, we're going to have a groundbreaking for the airport, so let's put that out there.' We'd do that kind of strategizing. This was new to me. I had never done that as a legislator."

Interestingly enough, Peña found the media situation in Washington somewhat easier than the one he encountered at city hall in Denver. Some of that was attributable to his own skills developed through eight years of unrelenting media coverage as mayor, but some of it he attributes to the fact that his federal department was covered by reporters who knew a lot about transportation and who, in his judgment, were a lot more balanced than at least some of the reporters he faced in Denver.

How, then, does a leader-manager put a press operation together that can both deal with the inevitable criticism that will be received and at the same time manage media relations in ways that further the organization's goals? Perhaps most importantly, a "point person" is needed to work with the media. This might be the leader-manager himself, although this adds a lot to the leader-manager's list of tasks, or it might be a communications liaison or other person in the organization. The point person must be fast on her feet, responsive, an excellent writer, and someone who gets along with the working press. She must be able to design communications strategies for major initiatives that are more than one-day stories. She must understand the electronic media as well as print and the growing impact of the Internet, as well.

Importantly, she must be an integral part of the agency or organization. She should be a part of the policy-making team and have general access to others on the team. She should regularly assess public opinion and its impact on the agency's operations and initiatives, and she must be an internal watchdog— all at the same time. This is the person who often picks up the first sign of trouble from aggressive and inquisitive reporters.

A point person is important, but ultimately all leader-managers in the organization need to be savvy with the press and supportive of the organization's communications strategy. In this regard, we encourage all leader-managers to observe some simple rules of the communications game:

1. Be fair, frank, and friendly.

2. Be accessible and get back to reporters as soon as you can. They have deadlines they must meet.

3. Look out for the "off the record" tag. Never say anything that you do not want reported. If you do not know all the facts, say so and get back to the reporter as soon as you can.

4. Be careful about deliberate leaks. They are dangerous, particularly if the word gets around that you are playing favorites.

5. Do not try to be an editor. Unless a press report includes serious inaccuracies, do not get into an argument with the media. As former governor Dick Lamm of Colorado once famously said, "Don't get into fights with people that buy ink by the barrel."

6. Work at the job of improving your TV presence and effectiveness. That means, however time-consuming it may be, that your presentation includes good lighting and locations and that you speak in understandable English in relatively short sound bites.

7. Never put anything in writing, including e-mail, unless you are prepared to see it on the front page of your leading newspaper.

8. Never, never, never lie.

8

Demonstrating Character and Integrity

Effective leader-managers are skilled in many ways. Most important, perhaps, is their ability to work with other people. As we have described in earlier chapters, leader-managers develop critical listening skills that help them learn from their own employees. Leader-managers pick and motivate staff that will carry an organization to its highest level of performance. Leader-managers build networks of support and collaboration within and across organizations. Leader-managers connect with the public through the media and a variety of communication venues.

However, these people skills are not the whole picture. It does make a difference who the leader-manager is *as a person*. A leader-manager's ability to connect with others is rooted in his values, personality, ethics, and life experiences. Those qualities of an individual are the foundation upon which the people skills are built; they are the building blocks of effective leadership and management. Employees are inspired when they see a leader-manager offer direction and purpose for an organization while exemplifying the qualities and accomplishments that are sought for all in the organization. As others have noted: "People first follow the person, then the plan" (Kouzes and Posner 2007, 15).

The personal traits or characteristics of a leader-manager are an important part of this foundation. Self-confidence, decisiveness, inquisitiveness, innate intelligence, and flexibility, for example, are traits often associated with a leader. As one student of leadership notes: "Leaders have those indispensable qualities of contagious self-confidence, unwarranted optimism, and incurable idealism" (Cronin 1993, 12). Another writer describes leaders as possessing "extraordinary energy, great stamina, unusual powers of concentration, and, above all, supreme self-confidence" (Goodsell 1992, 7).

Mick Trainor identified a number of these traits in his interview. In a military combat situation, for example, he highlighted the importance of courage, confidence, and calmness. "Troops in danger have to see you up front, sharing their peril. There are several key points here. First, there's the issue of physical courage. If your troops think that you're sending them to their death, and your ass isn't on the line, they're not going to do it. You have to be physically courageous in their eyes. Second, you have to be confident in their eyes. You need to look like you know what the hell you are doing, even though it doesn't make sense to them. And third, you have to be calm; they're watching."

"I'll give an example of this last point," said Trainor. "When I was with the British commandoes on exchange duty, I was late one day for a meeting with the battalion commander. I was double-timing to where the meeting was taking place. Across the drill field, I heard a British color sergeant shout 'Sir!' I stopped and he marched up to me, stomped to a stop, and saluted in typical Brit fashion—right out of central casting. I admonished him and told him that I'm late for a meeting and that he best have something important to say to me. And with this pained expression on his face, he said, 'Sir, I wish the captain wouldn't run; it makes the troopies nervous.' The troops are watching you all the time. If you show signs of being nervous, unsure, or of being frightened, it goes through them very, very quickly. They have to see you with them and that you're calm regardless of what is happening."

For most leader-managers, confidence is joined by motivation. Leader-managers want to succeed. Success does not mean simply to get by, but to excel. As Federico Peña reflected upon his time as mayor of Denver, he emphasized the importance of passion and determination in motivating him to succeed. "You have to have passion. You have to really care. That passion comes from one of two sources. Either you really believe in something and you want something to be done, or you're really angry about something and you want to change it or stop something bad from happening. My passion came from the first. I'm a doer. I like to get things done. That was my passion. Another key piece is determination. I don't know how many times in the [Denver] airport project people said, 'Let's stop it. This is never going to get done.' I said, 'No. No.'"

Mary Peters used the metaphor of a merry-go-round to highlight the importance of motivation and preparation to her success in the transportation arena. As Peters concluded: "I had many opportunities. My father, who was a tremendous influence in my life, told me that life is like a merry-go-round. Every time you go around you better grab a ring because you'll never know when the gold ring is going to get there. With a combination of being prepared and opportunities, I was able to grab a couple of gold rings as I went around."

John Catoe, while at DC Metro and before in California, described his passion for connecting with employees and encouraging them to "be the best." "Leaders have to believe," Catoe emphasized. "I believe that my job is not just to go in as head of an agency. You need to go in there and think that you're going to be the best that you possibly can be. I was talking to a group of students at a graduation ceremony this Saturday at a high school that I went to. I talked about the paths and the journeys that they're going to be on for the rest of their lives. And I said, as you make this journey, whatever you do—go to college, get a job, and whatever the job might be—always focus on being the best. If you focus on being the best in everything that you do, that's what's going to happen. You're going to achieve that and you're going to learn in the process and have much more satisfaction."

For Catoe, also, there is a deeply held belief in the power of individuals to achieve and succeed. Like most leader-managers, he possesses a passionate optimism and faith in the ability of his employees to move the organization forward at all levels. His own life story is one of achieving success from a very modest family background. "I want to articulate this in the best way I can. I think it's who I am as a person. I have never lost sight of where I came from. I totally understand the importance of every employee in this organization. My tendency is for a connectedness with those individuals in the 'lower level' jobs. From a pay standpoint they are lower, but they are just as important.

"It comes from my background," Catoe noted. "I didn't get into this for my ego. . . . I'm an employee of this agency just like the person downstairs cleaning the bathroom. I understand that I have a role that I have to play as general manager, but I'm not hung up on who I am. I get my enjoyment out of the success of other people; I know people can do it. Everyone has it in them. People want their organization to be great."

Leader-managers also possess a strong sense of purpose. Typically, they are driven by values and goals that are fundamental to who they are as persons. Tom Payzant explained that his "core values" revolved around his passion for and commitment to public education as a fundamental source of opportunity for all children. "I think the core values were with me when I started teaching. I wouldn't have gotten into this work at all if it weren't focused on kids. And then the experience in New Orleans [where he served as an administrative assistant to the superintendent] pushed me even further. Even before standards-based reform made it clear that education was for all kids, I would go back to the strong voice of public education and its importance to serve the common good in our democracy."

"Public education," Payzant continued, "is what should enable all students to access opportunity. It's the American story. We've had some bad chapters with pervasive achievement gaps and we're still not where we need to be, but that basically has been what's driven me throughout my career to try and move us closer to the ideal. Our focus needs to be on providing opportunities for all students to succeed. That's the American dream. That's public education. That's why it is so important for us not to lose sight of the common good argument."

Core values, to use Payzant's phrase, become the guideposts for action. Leader-managers develop a strategy based on their core values that translates goals into action. How do they move their organization forward? Payzant identified a "theory of action" involving teaching and learning that built upon his core values of equity and access to education: "Core values underlie a theory of action. Ten years ago I didn't even know the term 'theory of action.' I don't think it was around in the early 1990s, but since then, leaders are expected to have a theory of action. When you come into a new organization as a leader you've got core values and perhaps some goals, but what you need is a theory of how you're going to reach those goals and stay true to your core values."

"At a very simple level," Payzant said, "my theory of action, although I didn't call it that for a long, long time, has been about the people and the quality of instruction in the classroom. And I think the way I sharpened it in Boston relates to my focus on leadership development in principals. My theory of action is a laser-like focus on teaching and learning in the classroom and what you do to support teachers to get better at what they are doing. Importantly, you have to get the right people in the principalship to lead the work. That's basically how I've thought about it during the last decade."

For effective leader-managers, these various personal traits and values—self-confidence, passion, core values, and others—are combined with a commitment to high standards of integrity for themselves and the people who work for them. All the good intentions and leadership in the world will do little good if the agency or government that a public manager leads is perceived to have serious or even occasional ethical problems. One such problem can badly damage what may well have been an exemplary record of leadership.

Achieving and maintaining a high standard of integrity for yourself and your organization requires constant attention. Leader-managers who demonstrate the key practices we have been describing in this book are well on their way to leading a high-performing organization with high and consistent standards of integrity. In fact, the greatest safeguard against ethical lapses is that very sense of mission and esprit that all of our managers have sought to create in the agencies or governments they have led.

Nevertheless, our leader-managers—because they are *public* managers—have a special responsibility to take the setting of high standards of integrity and the implementation of those standards seriously. They must do this every day and every week that they are on the job and trying to provide excellent service to their constituents. They are, after all, spending the public's money, which has been extracted largely through taxation.

Private sector managers in firms with public subsidies may face the same pressures from the public and the press, as we have seen during the current economic meltdown, but for public managers, conducting themselves in a way that can meet intense, daily public scrutiny is an essential and expected part of the job. Not taking it seriously can lead to grief and, often, disaster in the face of what may well have been good performance. Plus setting those standards usually requires a clear understanding of the law and its effective implementation within the agency. All governments have anticorruption and conflict of interest laws. Understanding them thoroughly and how they affect an agency's personnel and operation is a critical part of a public manager's job.

That means, among other things, knowing where to get advice and counsel on important integrity issues. Many governments provide that advice as a matter of course through ethics commissions or in-house integrity offices. The important point is that public managers know who provides it and how to get it, whether the question affects just them or their employees.

Ethics laws and regulations are often confusing and may well overlap each other, depending on their source. Local officials, for example, may be subject to local ordinances and codes and to state ethics laws as well. Moreover, while federal ethics laws usually apply to federal agencies and employees, Congress has given federal investigators broad authority to audit and investigate suspected ethical violations in state and local governments that do not necessarily involve the use of federal funds. That is one of the reasons why so many state and local corruption investigations and prosecutions wind up in the Federal Bureau of Investigation and U.S. Attorneys' offices. In short, public managers whose agencies get in trouble may find themselves facing not only the local district attorney and the state attorney general but federal prosecutors and investigators as well.

For that reason, wise leader-managers make sure that they not only have a firm understanding of the integrity laws and regulations under which they operate, but also equip themselves to investigate suspected violations before prosecutors and their investigative teams come calling. The best way to do that is to create an in-house investigative and audit unit that engages in ongoing performance and integrity audits of the agency's operations or, in smaller agencies, to identify such a unit within the government they serve that is available to them if they need such services.

In Massachusetts in the 1980s, that took the form of a special investigations unit in the Executive Office of Public Safety. It was headed by a respected state police lieutenant colonel, joined by a captain and six troopers. They did background checks on key state appointees; they also had broad authority to investigate on their own as well as respond to public tips or complaints. Any state manager could call on them at any time. They not only helped to uncover inappropriate conduct and set the stage for disciplinary proceedings, but in some instances they developed cases that were referred to the state attorney general for possible prosecution. They were a built-in deterrent, but they also were very important to public managers who needed their help or who, in some cases, were unjustly accused of unethical conduct and were subsequently exonerated by this unit.

Legal standards are important, but they are not the only criteria when considering ethical integrity. Writing to fellow school administrators, Tom Payzant noted that "what is legal is not the only question. Ethics have as much to do with the appearance of something as with its legality. This does not mean that ethical judgments are superficial. Public officials are role models, like it or not. How we conduct ourselves in our offices is as important an aspect of the trust the public has placed in us as the decisions we make" (2004, 16). Payzant noted, for example, that "even though a gift might meet the legal test—that is, it does not come from a vendor or is not significant in value—it may not meet the ethical test."

That test, Payzant argued, is answered most often by the question, "Who benefits?" If a gift or contribution or service provides benefit to the individual manager, rather than the agency or school district for which he works, it raises a serious ethical issue, even if it meets a legal standard. Business funding for a conference to discuss school reform strategies benefits brings to the district, but complimentary tickets to a theater, regardless of their value, provide a personal benefit and raise ethical concerns. As Payzant concludes, "the litmus test, 'Who benefits,' almost always will rule out favors that might easily be construed as sweetheart deals."

As a final recommendation, Payzant urged full disclosure as standard operating procedure. "Whatever the gift, wherever the meeting, or whoever the opportunity comes from, the first rule of thumb is always public disclosure." Leader-managers should keep their bosses informed of any actions that bring benefits to them or their agency, and this information should be open to public scrutiny.

For all these reasons, every public agency needs a code of conduct that helps its employees to determine what they can and cannot do and provides them with guidance on the subject. A municipal or state revenue collection and enforcement agency, for example, faces numerous integrity questions that are unique to it. Can its lawyers handle legal work during their off-hours? Can that work include tax advice not connected to the employee's job? What can its accountants and auditors do professionally on their own time and in what fields?

Moreover, revenue examiners and investigators spend most of their time working on their own out in the field with individual or corporate taxpayers and their lawyers and accountants and usually have fairly broad discretion to make decisions about what is owed and how it will be paid. Settlements have to be approved by their supervisors, but those supervisors cannot be sitting at their elbow while they meet with dozens of taxpayers in order to determine a taxpayer's liability. Building inspectors work in a similar environment with a lot of discretion on the building site. The opportunities for improper influence and outright bribery in both cases are many.

Before the current emphasis on community policing, police officers patrolled neighborhoods largely in patrol cars and regularly rotated from district to district so they would not get too close to a particular neighborhood and be subject to corruption over time. More recently, Americans have begun to understand that if they want safe neighborhoods, cops must get out of their cars, walk their beats, and do everything they can to get close to their assigned neighborhoods and the people who live and work there. That means that they have a right to know what they can and cannot do. Can they accept a cup of coffee from the local breakfast shop as they talk to the owner and mingle with the customers? Can they accept an invitation to dinner from a local activist and her family, or free tickets to the local ball club provided by the owners for the officer and a group of kids from the neighborhood?

Codes of conduct should provide public managers and their employees with the guidance they need to do their job the way it should be done *and* in a manner that is consistent with the highest standards of integrity and that also recognizes the importance of the employee's judgment. The code should be developed in close cooperation with those employees and their unions, and it should require regular, in-service integrity training. Employees must stay current with changes in ethics laws and have an opportunity to raise questions and get answers to the kinds of issues that inevitably develop when they are dealing with a delinquent taxpayer or a gang that is terrorizing a neighborhood. Leader-managers should be able to ask for and receive official guidance and opinion letters, if necessary, if they suspect that they or their employees might find themselves in a situation that violates current conflict of interest laws or otherwise compromises their integrity.

Any leader-manager worth his salt will insist on thorough background checks for his employees as a matter of course before they are hired. How extensive those backgrounds checks are obviously depends on the nature and complexity of the job that has been posted, but at a minimum they should include making sure that the employee has paid her taxes, is not delinquent in paying traffic and motor vehicle violation fines, and has filed the necessary employee disclosure forms. The more sensitive the position, the more extensive the background check should be.

Because leader-managers work in an intensely political environment, there are many perils and pitfalls that, unless handled carefully, can compromise their integrity and that of their employees. How do they deal with demands from the chief executive's political organization while maintaining the commitment to integrity that is so important? What about the campaign fund-raising process? In Massachusetts, it is a criminal offense for an unelected public official to be involved in soliciting money for any political purpose whatsoever, but the Massachusetts law is not the law in other states. Can public managers be involved in the political fund-raising process? Should they be? What if they are asked to raise money from people or firms with which they or their agencies do business?

How much time should leader-managers spend with businesses or nonprofit organizations that are providing services under contract to their government? This question has grown in importance as governments increasingly contract for services across a wide range of activities. It may well be that under certain circumstances services can be delivered more effectively and efficiently by contracting for them with private or nonprofit entities. But when campaign time rolls around, political fund-raisers will invariably seek out contractors or constituent groups that have a strong interest in what you as a manager are doing or have done, and they ask you for help. Public managers who value their integrity had better get the ground rules straight in advance—ground rules that reflect the high standards of integrity expected of public officials. If those rules do not exist, leader-managers should make sure they do before the campaign fund-raising process begins.

What about lobbyists? They are everywhere, and while many of them are fine, upstanding people, they want you to do things that will benefit their clients or their organizations or their causes. The rules with respect to lobbyists are simple and clear. Be courteous. Listen to what they have to say—but accept nothing of value from anybody. Life will be a lot easier that way, and you will be able to do your job without fear or favor from anybody.

For obvious reasons, reporters and bloggers swarm like bees around news of real or suspected integrity violations. Reporters may or may not be interested in the great things you are doing to help people in need, invest in economic growth, or build a first-rate public infrastructure, but they will be on your doorstep in a minute if questions are raised about your ethics or the ethics of your operation. That kind of press coverage can wipe out months and years of solid achievement and follow you for the rest of your life.

The best way to avoid that kind of press coverage is to set the bar high and insist that you and the people who work for you meet that test. If, however, as occasionally happens, somebody who works for you is guilty of an ethical lapse, the operative rule is to make it public fully and completely before the press does. The experience will not be fun, but it will be a lot less disagreeable than if the media finds out about the employee's lapse first, or finds out that you knew about it and did not disclose it.

Any discussion of ethics and integrity must include the personal conduct that citizens have a right to expect of those who commit to public service. Recently, there has been a spate of incidents involving prominent public officials, both elected and appointed, who have engaged in unethical or inappropriate conduct in their personal lives. These incidents have raised serious questions in many people's minds about what public servants are made of and why they cannot seem to behave themselves. Occasionally, some prominent psychologist tries to explain that as people rise in public life, they begin to feel invincible or in a position where they do not have to pay attention to the rules of public or personal ethics. This is sheer nonsense. The more important the job, the greater the scrutiny; and the negative impact of such conduct on the wrongdoer's loved ones and on the reputation of public service itself is incalculable.

Such behaviors raise serious questions about the core values that drive a leader-manager. As noted in our earlier discussion in this chapter, the traits and values of a leader-manager form the foundation for ethical integrity. Federico Peña traces this to the family: "I think your personal integrity comes from your family. My parents raised six children, and they taught us to be honest, to be proud of your family history and background, and to be good people. So all my personal values came from my family, bottom line. I didn't have to learn about truthfulness or working hard or believing in myself; that all came from my family. I've always had that. I've always just naturally believed that you had to be a person of integrity at whatever you do. I've always believed that anybody who runs for public office should hold themselves up to a higher level of integrity than people who are not in public office. That's my own personal judgment and value system. If you're not willing to do that, then you should not be in public office. Period."

In short, it is not enough to know, understand, and follow the ethical precepts that Americans have a right to expect of public servants in their work. People in a position of political or public responsibility must understand that their personal and family life will also be the subject of public attention. That means that their personal life should reflect to the greatest extent possible a commitment to the kinds of values that most Americans admire and respect in their own daily lives. If the people who serve the public do not understand that, then they had better not pursue public careers in the first place.

9

Conclusion

This book grew out of our common commitment to education and public service. Both of us have dedicated our careers to making the world a better place through public service and helping others to do the same. The interviewees in this book shared our interest in developing effective leaders and managers to tackle the many problems and challenges that face our society.

Our discussions that shaped this book followed a number of paths, but there is one recurring question that was touched on in each interview: "Is there a difference between leadership and management?" Perhaps more explicitly: "Is there a *meaningful* difference between leadership and management?" We tossed that question back and forth as we shared our own personal experiences. For Michael Dukakis, thirty-five years in state government as a governor and legislator led to the conclusion that there is very little difference. For John Portz, on the other hand, ten years in a university at the middle levels of management and twenty years teaching about public administration left a different impression. Through the course of our conversations and our interviews with leader-managers, we found common ground. Yes, there are differences between leadership and management, but the differences are overshadowed by a set of common practices that form the heart of this book. We need public sector leader-managers who are effective in exercising these practices.

Our interviewees captured this perspective in their own words. Mary Peters, for example, saw clear differences, but started from the premise that you need to be both. "Let me go back to the question you asked earlier: 'Are you a manager or are you a leader?' I think you have to have some qualities of both, especially in the public sector. You have to have both attributes. But I think there is a difference. Right now, as the secretary of this organization [U.S. Department of Transportation], I am in a CEO position. My job is to be about 80 percent strategic and only about 20 percent tactical. I want to be charting the course of where we're going. What do we want to accomplish? What do we need to get us where we want to go? I need to stay about 80 percent strategic."

"My chief operating officer," Peters continued, "needs to be about 80 percent tactical and 20 percent strategic. You don't want to keep managers out of setting organizational strategy, but you want them to be the ones who are putting the plans in place to accomplish the objectives that you've set out. Having those objectives is very important. As with new contract officers and driving around to see projects, they need to see what we're going to do. People have to understand where they're going and why."

"The leader defines where the forest is," Peters concluded. "The leader defines where the organization is going. That's the role of the CEO. That's leadership. The manager makes sure that those trees are being chopped down efficiently and effectively. Focusing on the right goals is the role of the CEO. Working efficiently to accomplish those goals is the role of the COO [chief operating officer]. That's management."

Tom Payzant followed suit, portraying the leadership–management relationship as a continuum. "On one side of the continuum is leadership and on the other side is management. The two converge in the middle. Sometimes you function more in management, and sometimes you function more as a leader. At some point I think there is a lot of ambiguity about trying to make fine distinctions. I think of management more as learning a set of skills that focus on the work of technical change, improvement, and operations. Relationships and people skills are important, but not to the same extent as I think they are in leadership, where leaders must set the vision, core values, and strategies for the adaptive changes necessary to achieve desired results."

Mick Trainor was asked a question similar to what we asked all interviewees: "Were you primarily a leader or a manager?" His response was similar as well: "I don't think that anybody who's going to be successful can be exclusively one or the other except in a narrow sense. You really have to be both to be effective."

"In combat," Trainor noted, "you don't have to be a very good manager in the accepted sense. Leadership is what counts above all. Leadership skills involve being able to influence the actions of others. A lot of it comes from intuition, from experience, and from being very sensitive to interpersonal relations, and knowing human nature. You can be a very good leader and an absolutely terrible manager, because leadership is inspiring and getting people to do that which you want them to do even though their inclination may be just the opposite. Nobody wants to get out of a foxhole and charge through an artillery barrage, but a leader inspires his troops to do so despite the danger. A manager would probably analyze matters and stay put. That's why we have leaders in combat and not managers. Managers manage systems; they're managing things. They are far more analytical and far less intuitive. Leadership is intuition based upon training, mission, experience, and understanding of human nature. Leaders lead human beings."

Trainor concluded with a statement that captures the essence of our position: "You can't divorce leadership from management. They are different, but they are intertwined. It's a matter of emphasis as to which takes priority and that is dependent upon the circumstances. You can be called a manager without being a leader, but you're not going to be very successful. You can be a good leader without management skills, but you're not going anywhere either. To make your mark, you have to be both. . . . Whether it is leading or managing, it goes back to understanding people and developing people skills."

Ultimately, then, the country needs leader-managers—people skilled as both leaders and managers—to address the many challenges that Americans face as a society. This book does not have all the answers, but it has laid out a set of qualities and practices that we think are fundamental for successful leader-managers if they are to have a transformative effect on the lives of their fellow citizens.

First, leader-managers must be people who can reach out to those around them and bring them genuinely into the process of developing and implementing solutions to real problems. You want those involved to take ownership of the process and the outcome. As Mary Peters put it, there needs to be a "line of sight" that connects employees and their work to the goals of the organization. Many public servants have a passion for public service, but their strong feelings about the challenges they face may make it difficult for them to reach out to those who disagree with them on a particular issue. In fact, our students will often say to us, "Do we really need to bring these people into the process? They are probably opposed to what we want to do." On the contrary, it is precisely those who have doubts who must be brought into the process at the earliest possible time.

Leader-managers must be good listeners—a trait few people are born with. Most people who are deeply and actively involved in public life are good talkers. They feel strongly about the world around them, and they want to make it better. Furthermore, many of them like to talk, and, in fact, being a good and persuasive talker is an important part of communicating effectively in the public sector.

What they may not do well is listen carefully to the ideas and suggestions of other people—including people who, at least initially, may not share their concerns or their philosophy. As a leader-manager, you have two choices. You can deliberately exclude such people from what you are doing and win their undying enmity, or you can bring them into the process, involve them actively with others, and seek to incorporate their ideas and values into what you ultimately recommend. In fact, you may even learn things from them you never thought about yourself!

Surrounding yourself with excellent people who either have or, with your help, can quickly learn to develop the skills of good leader-managers is another critically important part of what it takes to be an excellent leader-manager. Busy leader-managers in the public sector must learn to delegate to people who share their vision and their commitment to public service. Finding such people is not easy—not because the world lacks well-intentioned people, but because good intentions simply are not enough if one is going to be effective in the public sector.

Nor is success in the private sector a guarantee of success in public life. Leading and managing in the private sector is not easy, but it does not involve confronting the bewildering array of elected officials, interest groups, and media that face public officials from the day they assume their positions. That is one reason why many private sector leaders fail when they move to public life. They are good at what they do, but they do not understand that making things happen in a highly charged political environment is a whole different ballgame. And dealing with the denizens of the press every day is often something they have never had to face.

Effective leader-managers also are skilled at designing and redesigning organizations that can best serve their goals. They understand the importance of creating an environment in which the people they hire and their colleagues can excel. Bringing the right people into the organization can be stymied if the very rules and practices of the organization create barriers and obstacles for employees. Leader-managers appreciate the challenge of designing an "org chart" with lines of communication and responsibility that maximize the contributions of each and every member of the organization.

Moreover, while public leader-managers have to be passionate about what they do, they must also be balanced and steady. In any important public sector job, there will be at least one crisis a day, and often more. Unless leader-managers have the temperament, the psyche, and the first-rate people around them that they need, they will not make it through one crisis, let alone a daily one.

Leader-managers, as we have seen, must set high standards of personal and professional integrity for themselves and the people around them. Doing so is not particularly difficult, and we have tried to suggest a number of ways in which leader-managers can be effective and meet those high standards. In the last analysis, there is one simple rule that should be an integral part of every public leader-manager's life, both professional and personal: Accept nothing of value from anybody except for your official compensation. Not only will you quickly establish a reputation for unquestioned integrity, but you will also sleep well at night.

Becoming an effective leader-manager is a life-long endeavor. It is a learning process in which mistakes will be made. You learn from the mistakes and continue to develop as a leader-manager. As you learn, you may reach the conclusion that you are no longer the best match for your current role. Although he did some great things at the Washington Metro, including moving 1.5 million people during the 2009 presidential inauguration, John Catoe reached such a conclusion after facing a period of criticism over safety-related and other organizational matters. As he wrote in his resignation letter to employees: "My skill—and the reason for my past success—has been leading through empowerment. Now, I feel that Metro is in a period in which a much more directive leadership style is needed" (Catoe 2010).

All of our leader-managers are optimists, as well they should and must be. Public service is no place for pessimists. Leader-managers believe that good people working together with the kinds of skills we have discussed in this book can truly make a difference in the lives of their fellow citizens. If they do not believe that, then they had better try something other than public service.

Finally, our leader-managers have a passion for public service. It is part of what Tom Payzant referred to as the "core values" of a leader-manager. They are dedicated to the work they do. Turning around the public transportation system of the nation's capital or Boston's public schools or a major city like Denver; trying to persuade the people of California that it is time for a health-care system that provides basic health security for everyone; building and rebuilding the nation's transportation system when everybody wants to improve it but few want to pay for it; transforming an aging state court system that badly needs modernization; and leading men into combat—these are not tasks for the fainthearted. They require courage, skill, energy, and the ability to get things done in a highly charged political environment.

The rewards will not be financial. In fact, if someone wants to make a lot of money, public service is not the way to go. But the personal fulfillment and satisfaction that come from service in public life and making a real contribution to one's community, state, or country are priceless. That is why our leader-managers serve, and that is why we hope this book will help to inspire and train a whole new generation of leader-managers who will devote their lives to public service at its best.

Interview
Transcripts

Kimberly Belshé

Secretary, California Health and Human Services Agency
Interviewed by Michael Dukakis
March 26, 2008
Sacramento, California

Dukakis—Thank you for participating in our study. As a leader and manager in the human services area, people think highly of the work you've been doing. Perhaps we could start with a little background on your path that led to this agency.

Belshé—I received a master's in public policy in 1987 at Princeton. My most important mentor there was Dick Nathan. He was the only Republican on the entire campus, from what I could tell. My fellow students at the graduate school as well as my fellow teachers and the administrators were strongly Democratic. But Dick was a moderate Republican and a great guy. He really helped to inform my thinking about my career. I faced an important question: Do I go back to Washington and take advantage of a Presidential Management Internship opportunity or come home to practice public policy in California? I knew I'd always come home to California. As a fifth-generation Californian, I went to school in the East knowing I'd come home at some point. I graduated from graduate school during the time of devolution of responsibility from the federal government to the states. Dick and I talked about different opportunities for people interested in public policy. He kept saying that the action is in the states. He introduced me to some folks in California who were developing a significant welfare-to-work effort called the GAIN Program. So I came back to California.

The GAIN Program was a really wonderful alignment of Republican and Democratic principles, values, and objectives. In California, the governor and legislature appropriated monies to hire consultants who would go into California communities and explain the program, its intended purpose, and how communities could participate. Consultants met with local people, including business leaders, and talked about the welfare-to-work program. Their job was to explain the basis of the public policy regarding welfare-to-work—what it hoped to accomplish and the profile of people on welfare—in an effort to break some of the stereotypes and explain how the public could benefit from the program. I was hired as one of those consultants.

I did a lot of public speaking before business leaders, community groups, and others. I talked about what welfare is and isn't; what the objectives were of this public policy; and how businesses can participate and benefit. In some conservative communities I'd get hooted and hollered at, even personally attacked. In some of our more conservative rural communities, anyone from Sacramento is viewed as suspect. People don't trust you.

I was twenty-five at the time, so it was a great learning experience. I learned a lot about a very important social policy. Perhaps most importantly, I learned about the importance of investing time and effort to engage the public in conversation about what government does and why. Legislators and governors typically pass a bill and move on to the next idea, but rarely make a systematic and thoughtful effort to engage the public in policy implementation. It was a great experience.

I also learned about how people can be treated inequitably unless they are purposeful and forthright. There were three of us hired for this job: a woman, a man, and me. The woman was clearly the governor's person; the guy was Assemblyman Art Agnos's person; and somehow I got in. I quickly learned that my two colleagues were being paid twice as much as I was. I demonstrated that I could do the job and do it well, so I asked for a pay increase. The deputy director of the department said if I thought I could make more money elsewhere, then I should leave. I did.

My time with GAIN was relatively short-lived, for the reasons I've mentioned. I accepted a position with the state legislative analyst's office, but before starting I realized I didn't like Sacramento. So I went home to San Francisco and accepted a position with Ogilvy and Mather in public affairs. I worked on an anti-tobacco tax campaign, and the state AIDS education campaign, which was one of the first in the nation. This job was important developmentally because it made me realize that while I appreciate how important social marketing activity is, I felt I was better positioned to contribute at the front end in terms of policy development. That experience led me back to elected officials and policy leaders.

Dukakis—Was it at that point that you began working for Pete Wilson?

Belshé—Yes, I was his legislative assistant in Washington, DC, on health policy. I expected that then-Senator Wilson would run for governor, be successful, and I would have the opportunity to come home. In fact, he was elected governor, and I came out a week after the election to work on the transition. Many people from the Senate office wanted to work on the governor's staff. But when Governor Wilson said to me, "Well, Kimberly, what would you like to do with your bright future?" I indicated I thought I would serve him best working in an agency rather than the governor's office. I was appointed deputy secretary of this agency, which was then called Health and Welfare. I served in that role for three years.

Dr. Molly Coye was Governor Wilson's first director of the Department of Health Services and stepped down in 1993. The governor asked me to step into that position, which I did at the ripe age of thirty-three. Was I ready for the job? No. Are you ever ready for that job? Probably not. It was then a 6,000-person department with an $18 billion budget overseeing and administering both our Medicaid and public health programs. I served in that role for the balance of the Wilson administration.

I think the world of Pete Wilson. He looks at competence, ability, and potential. He doesn't look at age or whether you have a bunch of initials after your name. I was one of the few health commissioners without an MD.

Dukakis—One question we're looking at is the difference or similarities between leadership and management. Do you consider yourself a leader or a manager?

Belshé—I see myself as a leader-manager. No doubt you'll get some similar responses from the other folks with whom you speak. Part of it is definitional. Often, people have definitions of leadership that are much like definitions of management and vice versa. I view my role as being part leader and part manager; I work to find the reasonable and responsible middle ground between the two roles. It's not all big vision and articulation of where we need to go, and it's not all micromanagement. I view my responsibility as the leader of this agency to be the person who articulates a vision and sense of purpose. I have a responsibility to be clear as to where we need to go as an organization, but I also need to engage my staff colleagues in the "whys" that underpin our jobs as well as the "hows" of getting there. A leader is someone who can lead the charge to advance the vision and goals.

Given California's challenges in recent years, a lot of my job has been about defense. We have put forward and been confronted by a lot of difficult proposals on both a policy and budget basis. Leading the charge and advancing and defending policy is an important part of my job—and taking the shots. On the leadership side, it's vision, purpose, and motivation of people to come together around common goals and objectives. I view those imperatives as quite distinct from management, which is more about the process to advance the vision, common goals, and sense of purpose. How do we marshal our forces? How do we direct our team in a way that accomplishes what we have laid out from a leadership perspective in terms of vision, purpose, and common goals? That is a big part of my job in concert with our thirteen department directors.

When I reflect upon my experience during the Wilson years, I think in some respects these jobs have changed. Even though I'm at a higher level, I sometimes feel I do more managing and am involved in more detail now than when I was a department director. This may reflect the general diminution in the internal capacity of government—a challenge not unique to California. Our legislature, for example, is now grappling with the full effects of term limits. We have non-competitively drawn districts dating back to reapportionment in 2000. We have challenges around campaign finance. These structural governance issues are significant in California and have contributed to a recently announced five-year, $15 million government reform effort co-chaired by Leon Panetta. Moreover, just as there has been a diminution of capacity on the legislative side, there has been a diminution of capacity in the executive branch as well.

Dukakis—How has that happened on the executive side? What is the reason for that diminution of capacity?

Belshé—Some of the issues have been around for a long time. For example, socially, these jobs in the public sector are not viewed as very meaningful. Indeed, the term bureaucrat is often seen as a pejorative term. Another historic truth is that salaries are not very competitive. Overall, with benefits, the package is better, but it's just not competitive.

The new truths happened earlier this decade when California went through tough budget times. The previous administration eliminated positions, froze hiring, and created/supported incentives to encourage people to retire from state service when they reach fifty-five years. However, that's when people are hitting their professional stride. They have been in civil service for twenty-plus years. They should be running agencies or serving as the operational number twos to policy leaders. Instead, a confluence of factors contributed to an exodus of senior managers. As a result, senior leaders, such as department directors and agency secretaries, have become involved in a level of management and detail that in a preferred world really should delegate to senior managers. I'm overstating it to make the point, but to your question of leadership versus management, there is a challenge for any leader to find that right balance and California's current circumstances make it particularly so.

Given these issues I've just described, including the problems of limited internal capacity, I sometimes worry that in my current job I'm involved in a level of detail that I really shouldn't be. But it's a function of our environment.

Dukakis—Do you like to manage?

Belshé—Yes, I like to be involved, working closely with our team. As the agency secretary, I'm at the top of the pyramid. I have a very clear sense of self and position, but as I say to my colleagues at the agency, we're not the ones who do the work. The people in the departments are the ones who are managing and overseeing the services and supports upon which millions of Californians rely. They're the ones who are administering the programs. They are doing the design and implementation. Yes, I like to manage, but I am very mindful that I'm at a high level, macro-level, of management.

Dukakis—Were you deeply involved in selecting your department heads?

Belshé—Absolutely. And I also worked with the governor's appointments unit. It's been challenging. We have a governor [Arnold Schwarzenegger] who doesn't care if an appointee is a Republican or Democrat. In previous administrations, governors cared about those issues. Governor Wilson appointed Democrats, but he took a lot of heat for that. So we were mindful of that. But this governor is not about party; he's about talent—who's the best and the brightest for a given position. So even though we have a large universe of potential candidates, we've had some challenges in bringing organization and focus to the process. The Wilson team was excellent on appointments; it was more like an executive recruiting firm. It was very much a partnership. At the agency, we ended up taking a lot of the initiative in identifying, recruiting, and recommending candidates. I spent a lot of time in the initial years talking to people, reaching out to people, and interviewing people. I did a lot of screening and making recommendations to the governor.

I enjoyed doing that and it's important. Recruitment is a great opportunity to build a team that shares the governor's and my goals for Health and Human Services and ensures that our senior management team's priorities align with those of the administration.

Those top-level appointments are my team. We have a handful of people from the Davis administration that were asked to continue to serve. Indeed, we have one director who was appointed by Governor Wilson. We didn't come in with the assumption that the Davis appointees had to go. The only two departments where I was clear with the current directors that they would be asked to leave were the two biggest departments—the Department of Health Services and the Department of Social Services. These departments are so important to the overall goals and agenda of the new administration.

Dukakis—Tell me about agenda setting. How do you set the agenda, particularly in the context of the governor? What's your role in this?

Belshé—There are two broad approaches to agenda-setting. One is a relatively systematic approach that reflects the governor's priorities and assessment of the policy landscape, and the second is a more haphazard, opportunistic approach to agenda-setting. We started with the first approach, although elements of the second also have played a role.

It was clear from my initial discussion in October 2003 with the then-governor elect what his primary health and human services interests and priorities were. One of the reasons that I took this job was because they aligned with my priorities. The principal priorities we discussed in that initial meeting were health coverage, particularly children's health coverage, and obesity prevention. Those were his interests, and they matched well with my own. We had a very good discussion. He had some definite ideas.

One part of the conversation that particularly encouraged me related to our discussion of obesity. I come to this issue from the vantage point of someone who had run the Health Department, which oversees the state's anti-tobacco program. California has led the nation in its anti-tobacco efforts. California has learned a lot of lessons, for example, about how to denormalize a behavior and how to change a community's norms and expectations. We discussed the history of the California tobacco control experience, the research to date, and my thoughts on the applicability of the anti-tobacco model to the obesity issue.

The governor very much connected with the construct of environmental change to promote individual change. In getting into more details around these issues, it was clear to me that he was someone who was very thoughtful and engaged and willing to look at issues from a pragmatic, problem-solving perspective rather than an ideological one. I see myself in a similar way. Working together with stakeholders and the legislature, we've been able to make good progress in both these policy priorities.

Dukakis—Have you added to that agenda?

Belshé—Absolutely. We started with those two issues, and then over the course of our experience working together other issues and priorities for this agency came to clear focus. There are three others I would highlight.

First is emergency preparedness. It became clear early in the administration that there were some real deficiencies in our state's readiness. We provided the governor with a series of briefings regarding the state's readiness which highlighted California's strengths and weaknesses associated with our preparedness in terms of natural and man-made disasters. As a result, informed by analysis of the data and assessment of gaps in our capacity, the governor proposed and secured major new investments to support our health-care system and its capacity to meet surges in demand.

Second, child welfare is a priority. It was very clear early on that the governor and first lady had a personal and policy interest in this area. The first lady was particularly involved in the early years. She was involved around the obesity issue, including a governor's conference in 2005. She has helped to connect me to people at the local level who are involved in these issues. There have been a lot of issues around home placements.

A third priority involves supporting seniors and persons with disabilities to live in the most integrated setting possible consistent with the U.S. Supreme Court's Olmstead decision in 1999. The governor, from a personal and family basis, has a keen interest in persons with disabilities and the provision of services and supports to promote their well-being and independence.

Setting agendas and establishing priorities have been the product of a confluence of personal and professional priorities of the governor and those that we, as leaders within this agency, have identified and brought to his attention. Through dialogue and engagement with the governor, he has recognized that these are issues that we really need to take on.

This interactive process—one where the governor has been clear regarding his priorities and where we have brought issues, data, and research to him—has resulted in the identification of the major initiatives that organize and focus our work. Is that a systematic, thoughtful approach or a haphazard, inchoate process? It's probably a bit of both. These priorities have not been the product of an agency-wide, systematic effort in which we all sit down to map out explicit goals and objectives and measurement tools. Individual departments have done strategic plans in the context of their work, but we haven't done that on an agency-wide basis.

Dukakis—How do you build coalitions? How do you reach out and bring people into a policy process?

Belshé—The health reform effort we've undertaken in the past few years is a very good example of this coalition-building challenge.

This started with building our internal capacity. In the summer of 2006, one of my recommendations to colleagues in the governor's office was that if we are serious about a comprehensive universal health proposal—for the governor to announce in January of 2007—we need to build our internal capacity. Already, we had spent quite a bit of time from a policy perspective developing "health care 101" briefings for the governor and his senior staff.

This really began back in 2005. We looked at the demographics of California's uninsured, the fundamentals of health-care financing delivery, different coverage plans, and other issues.

Early in the administration, one of my recommendations to the chief of staff and the cabinet secretary was that all of us—the governor, senior staff, and those in the agency—share a common foundation in terms of information. Recall that Governor Schwarzenegger came to this job with an unusual background. To his credit, he came to office wanting to take on really big, complicated, and difficult issues. Frankly, other politicians, with you being an exception in your capacity as governor of Massachusetts, look at health-care finance and step back—they don't step forward and lead the charge. He was prepared to lead the charge. I thought it would be helpful to get everyone on the same knowledge base. Our agency organized, with the director of health services and the director of managed health care, a series of briefings. The governor was very patient. It was already clear in some respects what he wanted to do, but he also recognized that having a solid foundation of information and policy analysis would be helpful.

By the summer of 2006, it was clear that the governor was serious about comprehensive reform and that the administration needed more capacity to get the job done. Even though this issue was a priority, we basically worked on it after hours and on weekends. There were so many other issues in play, crises to be managed, and issues to be led, we weren't making sufficient progress. I told the governor's office that we needed to build our internal capacity— we needed to assemble a team of individuals dedicated to comprehensive health reform. We hired a team of four people to work 24/7 on health-care reform. They were led by Daniel Zingale, who is Maria Shriver's [Governor Schwarzenegger's wife] chief of staff and one of the governor's senior policy advisers, myself, and the governor's cabinet secretary.

One of the team members focused on coalition-building. I knew that if we wanted to do the policy work, if we wanted to do the political work, we needed to have the resources and the assets to make it happen. We hired someone who could focus on external relations and engaging people directly. All of us were involved, but this really was his singular focus.

Herb Schultz, the external relations person, was everywhere around the state. He would go out at key moments to meet groups that were important to building the coalition. We also brought in other administration officials. It depended upon the issue. It depended upon the organization.

The governor played a critical role in coalition-building. He invested a significant amount of his time to the process. He was personally invested. At points along the way we had different objectives, so our coalition strategies would be informed by where we were at a particular juncture, but throughout, the governor was supportive. In January and February of 2007, I accompanied the governor and others around the state for town-hall meetings on health reform and other priorities of the governor. In the spring and summer, we would invite individuals and stakeholder groups to come in and meet with the governor, including consumer advocate groups and leaders in the business community. We met in sector-specific meetings that would focus on a specific issue, as well as meetings that would focus on broad reform.

The governor constantly was engaged, which was really critical to keeping people at the table. When you have the governor of the state of California, or any state, look you in the eye and say, "Your input is important, your participation is critical. We're going to get there, notwithstanding all the naysayers and things you're hearing from the critics about why reform can't possibly happen," it keeps people at the table. It keeps people engaged. If the governor calls, they will come. It was a very important piece to our coalition-building and policy development efforts.

The project was jointly managed with the governor's office and the agency. I oversaw the agency side, which included me, the agency, and the managed care office, which is in a different agency, but works very closely with us. Daniel Zingale led the effort from within the governor's office. It was not a conventional approach to leading and managing—to have the governor's office that involved, though it was appropriate, given the governor's designation of health care reform as his number one priority for 2007. Roles and responsibilities were more ambiguous than is typical. The four team members working 24/7 on health-care reform sometimes weren't entirely clear who they reported to. But since this was the number one priority of the governor, it was clear to me that this would require an "all hands on deck" approach in which the governor's office takes the lead and we serve as the principal policy advisers. To make something like this happen, it is as much about the politics and the tactics as it is about the policy. So it was a good complement of ability and resources.

The end point was a very significant coalition of support behind comprehensive health-care reform. However, I recognize that one of your questions relates to being successful. One can ask: "What do we mean by success?" If success is measured by legislative accomplishments, then we weren't successful. If success is measured beyond specific bills to include policy ideas, reforms advanced, and coalitions built, then we have had some important successes. I point to this coalition as an example because it involved many business leaders and a number of the large chambers of commerce from around the state actually agreeing that employers should be required to contribute financially to health care. This was an idea you advanced back in the 1980s.

Dukakis—And Richard Nixon in 1971 . . .

Belshé—At some point we will get there. Our coalition involved every health insurer, except one, supporting the idea of guaranteed issue. Insurers agreed to offer health care to everyone, regardless of preexisting conditions, and to support a cap on administrative costs and profit. The coalition included many labor unions, consumer groups, business leaders, and many medical providers. The hospital association was supportive of taxing itself to draw additional federal funds and increase coverage. As we continue our reform efforts, we're asking, "How do we sustain this coalition and find ways to build upon it but not compromise it?" It is an impressive group. It demonstrates that with the right mix of reforms, we can get traditional stakeholders to step outside of their comfort zone—as one of my colleagues says—to support significant policy changes.

Dukakis—What about the press? What has been your role with the press? How do you interact with the press?

Belshé—On a personal level, I don't feel as if I've had a bad experience, with possibly one exception when I was appointed the director of health services and my earlier work opposing the tobacco tax initiative came up. In editorial cartoons and elsewhere there were some very tough criticisms associated with that. But that comes with the territory. Everyone has the right to criticize what you may have done privately in the past as it relates to a current or future public assignment.

Professionally, it has been challenging. I've had the good fortune of working with a governor over the past four years who is extraordinary at attracting media attention. To accommodate the media, we've had to move many of his public speaking events out of the capitol building where governors have historically conducted press events to major auditoriums. Also, we have so many more media credentials today than we did in the Wilson years. In general, the governor has been successful in reinvigorating Sacramento media coverage of politics and policy.

Regrettably, a lot of the coverage is more about politics than policy. We work hard at engaging key reporters in health and human services. We try to develop relationships that support communication to get the information out in a timely way, so we're never accused of hiding the ball. We try to be as transparent as possible. Our health reform team has been very proactive at engaging the media around health reform. It was very much a partnership between Daniel and me. Typically, I was the one who did the public speaking and the media events either on my own or with the governor, including calls to editorial boards. Daniel would be the one taking or initiating the more political calls. Often he would be the person off-the-record, and I'd be the one on-the-record. We really tried to be proactive and aggressive with the media.

Dukakis—In an issue like obesity, for example, I assume there is a media strategy to get the word out in a positive way.

Belshé—Absolutely. There is media engagement in the day-to-day reporting of the news that tends to be reactive. Our Department of Public Health, for example, fields dozens of calls every day about food safety, water issues, and other public health concerns.

At the same time, there are priority issues, like those I've mentioned, in which we are more proactive. We have a positive story to tell, or administratively, we've taken an important step forward with a policy initiative. We'll do a press event and reach out to the media to solicit their interest and involvement. Also, we engage in paid social marketing media on a number of critical issues, particularly with our public health agenda, where we are working to change community norms. It's been very hard in our tight fiscal climate to invest state general fund resources, but we have partnered with non-general fund organizations such as the California Children and Families Commission to invest in obesity prevention and social marketing strategies targeting parents and young children. We've also utilized federal nutrition services block grant funding to develop social marketing strategies that focus on moms as the primary decision-makers in most households. Our anti-tobacco efforts continue to be very effective. These are supported through separate funding from the tobacco tax.

Whether in earned or paid media, the media is a key partner in communicating clear and consistent messages around California's health and human services priorities. Can we do better? Yes. I was reading the *Sacramento Bee* today and there was an article on obesity based on a press release we did yesterday, but it included information that was not accurate. We need to provide that reporter with the right evidence.

Dukakis—How much of your time is spent working with the legislature? On the health-care initiative, why couldn't you get some of those folks to help? You seem to have a governor who's a lot less partisan than most of us; does that provide an opening for more legislative support?

Belshé—A couple of points are particularly relevant here, some of which are unique to California and some of which are not. What's unique, or semi-unique to California, is that we are one of only three states that require a two-thirds vote to pass the budget. We are one of only a handful of states that require a two-thirds vote to raise a tax. In the absence of divided government, this may be a good idea. But it is a reality that gives significant authority to the minority, which in California's case is typically Republicans.

The nature of our legislative districts is another key issue. Here's the dilemma we face, and this is just my perspective, but I think it's shared by others. The way our districts have been drawn results in them being very "safe" for the majority party. What does that mean in practice? That means that when there is a primary—and we have "closed" primaries that are open only to those registered in the party—you have Democrats competing to be the most Democratic, and you have Republicans competing to be the most Republican. Each is appealing to their voter base that will come out in the primary election. If you're a Republican, the base is conservative votes. Republicans run in the primary on a no-tax pledge. When they win the primary, there is no competition—they are going to Sacramento. Democrats run primarily as liberals. We do not have a political middle in our capital—we really don't. We have very conservative Republicans and very liberal or progressive Democrats.

This played out in health reform in very, very challenging ways. We have Republicans already on record saying no to new taxes, notwithstanding what they hear from the business community. Many business leaders, like Steve Burd, president and CEO of Safeway, are champions of reform, including a minimum employer contribution. They also are hearing from small businesses that have a significant business interest in defeating reform. Democrats are on the other side of the continuum and are very much influenced by the activists in their primary, particularly unions. Unions have an extraordinary level of influence in our state legislature, disproportionate to their representation in the workforce. The politics play out in very, very challenging ways. In light of this, I think the governor is quite right to identify reapportionment as a priority.

Dukakis—I don't disagree with that, but you did make progress on the health reform initiative, although it didn't get past the legislature.

Belshé—It was an important advancement in terms of helping the insured better understand why they should care about the problem of the uninsured, and also how coverage and cost issues affect the insured and uninsurable. The 20 percent of California's population that is uninsured receive care, but uncompensated costs are shifted to the insured—something the New America Foundation equated to a "hidden tax" estimated at 10 percent of premiums. Hillary Clinton is talking about this as well. We also need to think in terms of access. The uninsured impact access for all to the extent our hospitals are struggling with the number of uninsured using emergency rooms as their point of primary care.

As for the legislative failure, you can talk to ten people in California who've been involved in this and get ten different answers as to why the Senate Health Committee rejected the governor's proposal. From my vantage point, it was policy, politics, and personality. But fundamentally, in many respects, it was timing. The critical timing revolved around the state budget deficit, the erosion of the overall economy, and a report by the nonpartisan legislative fiscal analyst that concluded that any health reform will be accompanied by some financial risk. The report created a major challenge. It identified risks in health-care reform, some of which we thought were legitimate while others really weren't. But no one in the legislature, including the Senate Health Committee, was interested in having a meaningful conversation about that report. Were the report and its assumptions factual and its conclusions responsible and relevant? Should California move forward? We didn't have that conversation. The report provided a point of focus for the media and the public. It raised the question: "Why are we moving toward a $14 billion health-care reform proposal when the state has a $14 billion budget gap?" It became easier to focus on the fiscal uncertainties than the policy approach and tradeoffs.

The divisions were ideological as well. Some very powerful unions were totally opposed, and some very important business groups were totally opposed. There were fundamental tensions in terms of the policy. Our Senate Health Committee chair is one of the state's leading advocates for a single-payer system. Governor Schwarzenegger's plan was fundamentally not about either extreme. It was not solely market-based and it was not solely government-based. It was purposefully about the middle. But, as I said before, there is not much of a political middle in our state capital right now. And I continue to believe that a health policy reform debate that is anchored in the extremes of the issue is a debate destined to fail.

Dukakis—The argument usually made to the more conservative folks is that employers who are already providing insurance for their employees are carrying a substantial additional burden in higher premiums that help pay for the uninsured. It is time to get a level playing field. That argument didn't work?

Belshé—I'd love for you to ask them. It didn't do it for them in part because the business community was divided. While there were a handful of small business organizations that were supportive, generally speaking, small businesses actively opposed reform. That being said, I should note Safeway's Steve

Burd led a coalition of employers who provide coverage to employees today and who advocated for a minimum employer contribution—recognizing the governor's principle of shared responsibility and the economic benefit of a more level playing field.

We tried to accommodate small businesses. We made exemptions by size of the payroll. The governor's plan began with a 4 percent fee for non-offering employers. Through negotiations with the Speaker, the governor modified his approach to employer financing to require a sliding scale contribution, from 1 percent to 6.5 percent of total payroll depending on the employer's payroll size. Any way you structure it, you're creating incentives either to not increase payroll or not hire more people—those were the concerns we heard. But again, in terms of policy advancement, I think it is significant that we had so many businesses step up and acknowledge that employers did have a responsibility to make a minimum financial contribution to employee health care.

Every state is different. In your state, it's striking to us that in Massachusetts' recent health-care reform, labor was supportive. The employer penalty was minimal, but it set a policy precedent. I called John McDonough to help me understand the logic. We kept hearing that labor felt it was a really important policy precedent, even though employers in Massachusetts were already paying.

Our employers had no obligation. Democratic leaders put forth a proposal that was financed exclusively by employer fees. Why? Because their legislative counsel told them that by structuring it that way, it didn't need a two-thirds vote. It was a fee, not a tax, which in California requires a two-thirds vote. Again, it goes back to some of California's rules. Democratic leaders had to jerry-rig their reform proposal around the employer/payer provisions and the revenues they could raise with a majority vote. It was a significant burden on business, but it still wasn't enough to cover everyone. Our governance issues really were and continue to be significant.

In the end, leadership matters and gubernatorial leadership matters the most. Governor Schwarzenegger has an unyielding commitment to the issue of universal coverage and cost containment. That is why health reform got as far as it did. As someone who has toiled in this policy issue for many, many years, it is very disappointing to see the Senate Health Committee, led by Democrats, defeat the measure. It was a lost opportunity.

Dukakis—Any last comments?

Belshé—As a final note, those of us in senior or middle-level public management jobs need help from a capacity-building and succession-planning perspective. When I think about our legacy, certainly I hope there are legislative accomplishments over time and policy accomplishments as well. But I would hope that at the end of my tenure I can point to people accomplishments as well. I'm referring to my ability, and my team's ability, to recruit and retain really smart and dedicated people, from senior managers, such as department directors, to people like Peter [a current staff person] from the executive fellows program. When we get a good person in the agency, we need to talk with him or her about the future. Tell them: "Don't run off to law school or some other graduate program just yet. Let's see if we can find a job in state service to give you more exposure to public policy."

John B. Catoe Jr.
General Manager, Washington Metropolitan Area Transit Authority
Interviewed by Michael Dukakis
June 12, 2007
Washington, DC

Dukakis—In our study of public sector leaders and managers, one question we're interested in is your perception of leadership and management. Is there a difference between being a leader or a manager, or are they more similar?

Catoe—There are differences between a leader and a manager. A leader in my judgment paints the big picture. We're going to take that hill, and we're going to be the best in doing that. And we're going to accomplish that goal. A manager has to come back and say, "Here are the steps," and to make sure that from a tactical standpoint the goals can be achieved. The organization needs to meet every one of those steps. A manager has to manage that process.

As a manager, you shouldn't have to micromanage. If you find yourself micromanaging, then you have the wrong people in the job. A good example of micromanaging came this past week when a pipe burst in the air conditioning system on Wednesday at a station near Farragut North and DuPont under Connecticut Avenue. Our facility maintenance crew responded, but in the afternoon the head of that group came to me and said that representatives from the utilities company can't come out until Monday. Utilities people tell us where the wires are. Well, my head split open. I started to micromanage by telling him to call this person in this office and that person in the mayor's office. We had someone come out that afternoon and had the work done the next morning. That's micromanaging. When that happens in an organization, you have to look at who you have on the job. The manager is the person who makes the tactical decisions about what's getting done. The leader is the more strategic person, looking long-range and where the organization is going to go.

Dukakis—Put this in the context of your work in Santa Monica, before coming to Washington. Which were you doing there?

Catoe—Yes, I was doing both up to a point. The transportation system in Santa Monica was an organization, like a lot of government agencies, with outdated management. Basically, getting by was OK. There was little sense of looking towards excellence and quality-added service. My job was to manage the tactical focus of the organization, the manager's day-to-day work, what we're going to work on. I wanted people in the organization to understand the priorities from a day-to-day standpoint so the system keeps working.

From the leadership standpoint, we started to change process, and we focused on who we were going to become. I like to do this. When I went in there, I told the city council in my first month that we were going to become the number-one transit agency in the nation. People looked at me like I had been smoking something. The point is, from the leadership perspective, you have to paint the picture on the go. So I was managing from a day-to-day standpoint, but I was also pushing the aspect of where we're going to go with the public outreach, elected officials, and the community. That's the leadership role, and the day-to-day was making sure the buses got fixed, that they were pulled out and cleaned. After three-and-a-half to four years, I worked myself out of a job from a management perspective; I no longer had to manage. I was doing more of the leadership things, and the organization achieved an award three times. Finally, I found it was time for new leadership. So, yes, I did do both.

Dukakis—Let's go back to the issue of vision. You said that when you came to Santa Monica you wanted this system to be the number one in the country. Where did that come from?

Catoe—It's because I believe in that. I think leaders have to believe. I believe that my job is not just to go in as head of an agency. You need to go in there and think that you're going to be the best that you possibly can be. I was talking to a group of students at a graduation ceremony this Saturday at a high school that I went to. I talked about the paths and the journeys that they're going to be on for the rest of their lives. And I said, as you make this journey, whatever you do—go to college, get a job, and whatever the job might be—always focus on being the best. If you focus on being the best in everything that you do, that's what's going to happen. You're going to achieve that and you're going to learn in the process and have much more satisfaction.

Dukakis—Where did that sense of belief and vision come from? You once talked to one of my classes about your dad, who was a cab driver. Did it come from him?

Catoe—It came from a combination of experiences, and it really started off with negative experiences. I was very shy. I graduated at the bottom of my class in high school; then I went into the military reserves. Fortunately, that was one of the best things that happened to me. I met people who had different standards. I had grown up in a community in the projects in which the goals and expectations were very low. Now, I was meeting people who had high expectations; that began the change process. I went back to high school; people complimented me about finishing high school. I went on to various jobs, and I focused on those jobs. I realized that I wasn't a dummy; I was a pretty smart guy. Also, I liked the compliments. I liked achieving things. I don't like just going there and getting things done.

This perspective began around my mid-teens. It was just a little, but it started growing and growing. It wasn't the military per se. It was the people I met in the military. I met two guys who I befriended—Leo Cyr and Bill Perlee. One's dad was a vice president with a company, and the other's dad was an ambassador. They were totally different people from me. I talked to them about their lives and their backgrounds. And I looked at that and said, "That's what I want to be." That started me in the process, and throughout my career I've enjoyed watching the success of other people.

It isn't me going in and doing everything; it's me creating the environment in which people can perform. I fundamentally believe that people come to work to do a good job. They don't wake up in the morning thinking how bad I can be today. I identify people who I think have high potential, and I put them in jobs of responsibility. I listen to the input they give me in making decisions. I don't just listen to my managers. I go out and talk to people. I talk to the mechanics and other workers, including supervisors, because these are the people that can tell you what's going on.

Dukakis—Tell me more about those conversations and meetings. How do you do that? Do you make regular visits to employees in the agency?

Catoe—I do. Ninety-nine percent of the time I ride the system going to and from work. Whenever I arrive at a station, I always go to the station manager and shake his or her hand and ask how things are going. I also look for employees of the agency, such as the person cleaning the station, or a mechanic who's waiting for an assignment. I just go up and talk to them, asking questions.

Dukakis—Do they give you feedback? Do they feel intimidated by you because you're the general manager?

Catoe—Not anymore, it doesn't intimidate them. They give me incredible feedback about different issues and processes. The work-order process is an example. In this process, we have a group from operations that comes to a station to fulfill a work order. One station manager told me about a case where the work group came to replace tiles on one level in the station. The station manager approached the crew and said he had a similar problem downstairs. The operations guy said he doesn't have a work order for downstairs. So he comes back a week later, just to replace the tiles downstairs. This process is wrong. We rate a manager on how many work orders he gets done, versus the outcome. What's the outcome from a system standpoint? I heard about that from talking to people.

As another example, we were ready to make some decisions about putting square tiles in the stations. One guy said, "Have you ever laid tiles 600 feet? You can't lay them straight. It's going to look like you came from California smoking stuff." Well, we're not laying square tiles anymore. That's from talking to people.

The key is letting people know you're listening *and* then doing something about it. It's easy to just listen, but you'd better enact some of those things you hear about. You've got to come right back and get your managers together. Tell them, "Jim, I want this done and I want this done. I want to fix it." When employees see that, they talk to you, and action occurs, then they'll start talking to you more. You're beginning a process now. They're giving you feedback. You know things can happen. I get dozens of e-mails. I give out my e-mail to employees directly. The next step is, again, tell them where you're going to go. Paint a picture of where we're going to go. And they start believing some of it.

There are about 10,000 employees in the Washington Metro, and I communicate with all of them. I do a weekly, and sometimes three times a week, memo from me as an e-mail to every employee in this agency. Every event that occurs, our employees know about it before it gets to the newspaper. Every time we have a board meeting, I tell them what's going to the board. After the meeting, they'll know exactly what the board did. When we have shifts in the organization, they know about it beforehand. The funding issues, they know about them. For the layoffs we had to do, I must have had fifteen meetings with employees to say, here is where we are, here are the steps, here is what will happen to those individuals who are laid off. I did this not only verbally but also in writing. We took care of them, not only from the standpoint of severance, but we walked them through the process of the transition.

Every manager who was involved with the layoffs was trained about the humane way of doing this. We told them, "You're going to meet several individuals. How are you going to talk to them? What forms are you going to use? How are you going to follow up? Explain the reasons." There needs to be a compassion aspect. Layoffs are troubling things to do, but this one occurred without one complaint from employees, except for one seniority issue, from the standpoint of how they were treated. They knew "why" before it happened. They knew "when." They knew what the outcome would be and how we were going to follow up.

In general, we communicate with employees in a number of ways. We have a website that is used. Employees can write in. They can send e-mails directly to me. They don't have to send it to somebody else. I have a staff person take those and I want to know what the responses are. I won't accept a response that says, "We tried that before and it didn't work." I want them to really work on it. And I go out to meet our employees. I have one more location to go to. I've been to every location that we have; I've been to every facility. We meet for one and a half hours to three hours in sessions with employees, talking about who I am, where we're going to go, and what the issues are. Then I ask for questions. If their question is a specific grievance, I say that I can't answer the question. You should talk to your manager. I will be honest. I will answer questions, and if I don't know the answer, then I'm going to tell you that. I'm not going to lie to you. You're not going to like what I say sometimes, but I'm going to be honest with you.

We get good participation and feedback. It's always that first question. I don't want to be a schoolteacher here and pick people out, but once that first question comes, then it just really expands.

Dukakis—You seem to have an instinct for this. Where did that come from? A lot of managers, both public and private, have great difficulty understanding the importance of bringing their employees into the process. Did you learn it from somebody? Is it instinct?

Catoe—I want to try to articulate this in the best way I can. I think it's who I am as a person. I have never lost sight of where I came from. I totally understand the importance of every employee in this organization. My tendency is for a connectedness with those individuals in the "lower-level" jobs. From a pay standpoint they are lower, but they are just as important.

I think this comes from my background. I didn't get into this for my ego. This Saturday I was talking to a woman who graduated from high school a couple of years before me. She was referring to people of "our level and class," meaning upper level of society. I just started smiling because I'm an employee of this agency just like the person downstairs cleaning the bathroom. He or she is an employee of this agency and I've never lost sight of that. I understand that I have a role that I have to play as general manager, but I'm not hung up on who I am. I get my enjoyment out of the success of other people; I know people can do it. Everyone has it in them. People want their organization to be great.

I talk to people about all the negative press we've been receiving. I go out there and people stop me and ask, "What's going on at Metro?" I've been asked by several people, "Are you sorry you came here?" The answer is "No." What I want is to go home or go to the grocery store wearing a Metro shirt; then people come up and say, "Hey, how do I get a job there? That is a great organization."

That's what I want this to become. Who wouldn't want that? You think about it as one of the basic aspects of living—to feel good about what you do. I always say this in response to those who may not feel good about what they do, but are still connected to the mission of this organization, which is to provide transit services at the top level possible. I tell them, "We're going to get there." I tell them that in three years we're going to be voted the number one property in North America. I said it to them, and I said it publicly. I know we're going to get there.

Dukakis—You were in Los Angeles when the current mayor was elected. A big issue was school reform and a much stronger role for the mayor. Here's a guy that seems to have good people skills; people respond to him. He was ringing doorbells for me in 1988 when he was a young organizer for the teachers' union. He came out of the teachers' union and they endorsed him. And yet, within a matter of weeks, the teachers' union and the mayor's office were in sharp disagreement. How do you explain it?

Catoe—First, I think that the educational system—the public educational system—has some great teachers who are wonderful people who will do the right thing, but we don't pay enough.

Second, we have gotten away from the individual. We should be focusing on individual students, saying that each can be great. Instead, we've become more statistical, looking at the larger number and the process. We've standardized the process to the point that it's rubber-stamped; there's no deviation away from the program. With the new web, every teacher has to get the new web. With a new textbook, everyone has to have the same textbook. Teachers have to follow the same process, but that's not how people learn. People have different ways of learning and it's not focused on that.

And third, education has become so bureaucratic from an administrative standpoint. If you look at superintendents and other top administrators, everyone came up from being a teacher. That's not good for any organization, no matter what it does. You need some outside influence and a different approach to doing things. You need people asking questions about how things are done.

Dukakis—The unions are important in education, and they are important in the transit industry as well. In the recent collective bargaining process in Los Angeles, before coming to Washington, you said there wasn't going to be a strike. You said it was going to be a productive negotiation, and it was. How did that happen?

Catoe—Again, if you communicate what the outcome is going to be, people start thinking that it is their outcome. I kept communicating "no strike," and we were going to settle before the contract expired. All the experts were telling me what happens when you do that. The union is not going to go for that. I communicated it to the point that it wasn't just my expectation; it became the organization's expectations. We would be settled by that day. They might have said that we can't make it, but that was the day. It was planted in their mind: there's not going to be a strike. I kept saying it over and over again. People started believing that there's not going to be a strike.

So when we went into negotiations, the biggest piece was the board. That is, convincing the board that, first, we need more money, and second, they need to give me full authority. I can't be coming back and asking the board if I can do this or that. Here are the parameters; give me full authority to do that. I did get full authority. When we met with the union, we came loaded with information about national averages, where we were, etc. I told them, "We're lost; we're too old in comparison with the rest of the country." It shocked them. I gave them all of the information we had. I didn't hide anything; it was a different approach.

I can tell you in the beginning, the transit drivers' president was doing his normal style of shaking his finger and raising his voice. I just sat there and started smiling at him. One time when that happened, he said, "Why are you smiling like that?" And I said, "James, because I remember my minister in church. He was just like you. He was good. He would give a sermon with his finger shaking. Next thing you know, the collection plate came out. I've worked with you before." He never raised his finger at me again. He started to go and he would stop. We ate together, and we started to talk about our families together. We got to know each other.

But the key was I told him they were getting an increase. I'm not here to take things from them, but it has to be within the national average. You're not going to get increases beyond that. I'm not here to take stuff from you, but you've got to understand where we are as an organization. From a productivity standpoint, I need your help. It worked. We'd never walk out of negotiations. We had someone with us who facilitated and gave us both feedback. She had a union background, so the union trusted her. It worked.

I think it's all people stuff. It's like being an elected official. You can be the smartest person in the world. Look at Jimmy Carter; he was not effective because he was too hands-on. He didn't have the people with him. I always say it's the people. I tell people that I'm in this job not because of the money, but because the organization has a lot of good people who work really hard. I made sure they have a really good work environment, and as a result we are successful, and over time I moved into different positions.

Dukakis—How do you pick the top people in your organization? When you move into an organization like this and you start putting together a team, how do you do it? Describe that to me. When you came to Washington, did you bring some people from Los Angeles?

Catoe—Yes, I did bring some people from Los Angeles. However, the first thing I did was assess the existing management team. I met with them individually and as a group. I looked at the areas with a lack of performance and also successful performance. There was only one area that I would rate at the top, and that was security and law enforcement. A top-notch person handled this area really well. I started looking at the other people and the issues. We had two members of the executive team who the board had influence in appointing; they were awful. I made it clear with the board in my contract and in discussions that that's my job. You hold me accountable for the staff, but they work for me, not for you.

For those two individuals, I assessed performance based on the areas in which they were responsible. But it was not just my assessment. It was the assessment of the rest of the management team and outsiders who work with them. We can't get anything from them. We never get an answer. Nothing happens. They offer great talk and concepts, but there's no implementation. I fired them both and got them out of the way because they were an example of "no one cares."

I replaced them with people from inside the organization. They were people who had good skill sets and had a passion for the job. When I talk to people who might work for me, I want to feel passion for what they do. If someone tells me they have thirty years' experience, I'm not impressed. In fact, that could be a negative. "Why are you at that level with thirty years' experience?" Are they willing to go through a process? Are they willing to take risks? Can they say, "I know we do it this way but I think we should try this." When I hear that, I light up and I appoint those people even though they might not be the most senior. They demonstrate the most passion and willingness to try something different.

And so I did that with Sarah Wilson as my chief of staff. I figured her out my first week here. She was at a third level in government relations. I made her chief of staff. Now she's in charge of government relations, marketing, and communications. She's good, in her mid-thirties, very smart, and understands where I want this agency to go. She's working to do that.

May Polly Hanson was promoted. She was a police chief and now she's responsible for safety. The police chief reports to her. We had to let go the previous head of safety. He was a good talker. He described how we killed two people in accidents who were our employees. And we killed three people in February who were pedestrians. His approach to what we're going to do is to give flashing red lights to customers so the bus could see them. And his other idea was to put lights on the top of the bus. But he said nothing about training, about pedestrian safety, about reconstruction of accidents to find out why. Just no depth. He was a good speaker about accidents, but not a person who can change the culture of an organization.

But getting back to your question, I look for passion. I look for commitment. I don't care what kind of background they have. One person I'm bringing to Washington, Angela Burnside, is coming to head up human resources. I found her when I started in Los Angeles. I asked the head of the planning unit there, "Who is your smartest person?" We found Angela. She did some operator training and board work for me; she was a good communicator. I used her as a strategist. She did the research that prepared us for collective bargaining negotiations. I'm bringing her to Washington to head human resources, even though she's not a human resources expert. But she understands people, and she has played a major role in labor relations. She had labor relations and organizational development experience in Maine. I don't want a human resources expert who always tells me, "You can't do that." I want someone who's going to look at it from the perspective of how we make this place a great place for employees. What are the things we need to do from that perspective?

It's the employees who are going to make this agency great. It's the driver who drives the bus faithfully and speaks to the customers to start a relationship. It's the person who wants to make the train a little bit cleaner who is going to make this a great organization. And it's the supervisor who understands that their role isn't to write someone up, but to help the system and the service operate correctly. That's what's going to make the agency great, and that's what we're going to focus on. I'm looking for people who understand that.

Dukakis—Since coming to Washington, you've faced some negative publicity about the Washington Metro. How have you dealt with that?

Catoe—Yes, there were three fatalities in February, and we face overtime costs of $91 million that jumped 56 percent in five years. Those overtime costs are built into the employees' retirement fund. Also, we've had fires in the subway, not in the trains themselves but in wires that have been there for thirty years, as well as in trash areas. There was a bus that had a rear tire catch on fire. In fact, there was an editorial cartoon in the *Post* that had a big banner over the subway—Welcome, John Catoe—and smoke coming out of the subway. There are firemen running in and there's a bus on fire.

I have taken every opportunity in front of the camera, talking to reporters, going on TV, attending community meetings, and saying, "Here's what we're going to do." We're having community meetings every two weeks, around town, throughout the district.

I'm getting a lot of good feedback. The biggest thing I've received, which is helping me a lot, is the public. I really believe that the public wants me to succeed. Growing up in Washington and coming from the background that I do, I've had people say, "I'm praying for you." And I say, "I need your prayers." Every day I meet five or six people in the system who come up and say, "I see you in the paper and I'm praying for you." And I say, "Keep it up. Keep it up. We need it." And I assure them we're going to fix it. We're going to fix it. And the other piece is, I'm not going to embarrass you. I'm going to make you proud of the system and of the things we're going to do.

Dukakis—In terms of governance, you're in a complicated situation. You have a number of constituencies. There are four governments at least—Maryland, DC, Virginia, and the feds—and the public. How have you managed this environment?

Catoe—Yes, it is complicated. We deal with all those constituencies on various issues. And they all have representation on the Metro's governing board. In that regard, Maryland is probably the easiest jurisdiction to deal with. None of their members of the board are elected officials. They are all appointees of the governor. While they take direction from the head of the Department of Transportation in Maryland, they have some latitude to make decisions, and they're not political decisions.

In the District, two board members are city council members, another is the head of the transportation department, and another is a retiree who worked in city government. They are more political.

In Virginia, everyone is an elected official. Three are members of the county board of supervisors, and one is the mayor of Alexandria.

My job is to meet all of these folks. Recently, I had a one-and-a-half-hour lunch with Jim Graham from the District of Columbia, who is the chair of the board. He had been very critical of the organization. But he's turned out to be the best board member to work with. I respect him. I treat him with honesty. I follow through with him. I spend time with him.

He's also chair of the finance committee of the Metro and the District. I go to all of those meetings. Every time they contact me about a meeting, I go. He said, "You know about the committee?" I said, "Oh yes. This is important. You're important, and as the chairman, I want to be here." The general manager before me did not do that. The staff would brief board members. To me, when you have a board, you have to be there. You'd better know what's going on and you'd better listen to the issue. It's got to come from the general manager's mouth. Board members will question staff and look at you and say, "We expect you to do A, B, and C." It's showing respect. They're my board members. I need to be there. It takes a great deal of time, but it's important to do. I treat them all that way.

The other lesson I learned years ago is to help them work together. When they criticize another board member, they may ask, "What do you think?" I say, "I'm here to listen." It's not my job to say something about a board member. They know I'm not saying it about any other board member. I'm not saying it about them, and that helps the relationship.

Dukakis—What about Capitol Hill—is that an important part of your life?

Catoe—Absolutely. I meet with staff and committee chairs. Earlier today I met with Sherman Thompson, from Illinois, of the Appropriations Committee, about homeland security and a related appropriation for security. There were five of us in the meeting. He was talking about his bill. I want to do things with him and have him over here. I see my role at the Metro as establishing not only a professional relationship with members of Congress, but also convincing them why this agency is different. I tell everyone why we provide services to this region. We reflect the nation from an international standpoint. For people who come from all over the country, this is their system and it must reflect greatness.

There are two pieces to that. One, it motivates our employees. I believe in that. And second, I'm telling Congress that you can't treat us like any other system; we're different. We are a reflection of you. This needs to be the showcase.

But right now, I've got to tell you, and I've said this to other people, I'm embarrassed. Every time I ride the system there's a part of me that is really ashamed about the way our trains look, and the way we've allowed the system to deteriorate over the last thirty years. We're going to fix it. It won't happen next week. It won't happen next month, but in the next year, year and a half, to two years we're going to fix it.

When I tell employees that, they understand and they start coming up with ideas, too. You tell me how we can clean these cars because when I came here, we had not washed our rail cars in two years. We shut down the washer because that wasn't important. We were not in compliance. We had a firm that would hand-wash cars, but it would take almost a year and a half to cycle all of the trains through. Somehow, that wasn't important. It was not a priority of the organization.

Dukakis—Do you meet on a regular basis with your union leadership, formally or informally? How does that work?

Catoe—I've had multiple meetings. During the four months that I've been here, I've had eight or nine meetings with the union. We met on safety and had a joint press conference about the safety of the system. We talked about the things we're going to do. We kind of held hands and said this is going to be a joint effort to move forward. We met on issues of lack of responsiveness, what I saw as a violation of the collective bargaining agreement. I was stunned that the union allowed us to do it. They kept complaining, but nothing happened.

We're going to have a whole new approach to labor relations. Our labor unions have my cell-phone number, my personal cell-phone, my home number, and they know when they call that I take the call and address the issue. They're asking, "Where are we going to go?" I've painted the picture to them where we need to go, but I can't do it alone. They have to be a partner.

We have five unions. We have a monthly meeting, but we'll meet more often if there are issues to discuss. We don't talk about grievances, but about issues and processes.

Dukakis—In general, how do you set the agenda for the Metro? A broader vision, which you've mentioned, is certainly part of that. You also must deal with specific events, some of which put the agency in a negative light.

Catoe—Yes. But a lot of it is on the basis of values. What are the values and vision for the organization? And then, you start looking at where the roadblocks are; what's stopping us from getting there? When you see cars that are dirty and other problems, someone is not focusing on quality of service and customer service. This town is probably the most publicized transit town in the nation. I have been on TV more in the last four months than in the five or six times in my entire career before coming here. I'm in the newspaper and on TV at least once a week, if not several times a week.

Transit is very important to this region. When you listen to people talk in restaurants, when they're waiting to be seated, they start talking. I remember once, when a person hadn't seen another person for a long time, they described where they were living by the nearest Metro station. Another time, people would say, "Yes, we took Metro to get here." That's the only way to get downtown. When you hear that from the public, you know that they appreciate the system. They see it as their system. We're fortunate to have that level of interest.

The *Washington Post* has a reporter who gives front-page coverage a lot. Her entire job is Metro; that's all she does. So the *Post* plays a role in setting the agenda. The publisher is Donald Graham. His mother was Katherine Graham, who owned the *Post*. My mother worked for her. My mother was the person who made sure the menu was correct in the executive dining room. We talked about that; that's how we opened one of our meetings. It was an emotional experience for both of us. My mother was very close to Katherine Graham from the standpoint of a personal connection. We talked, in front of the others on the executive board, about what our mothers would say now. Look where their sons are. We connected emotionally. And I said, "Where are we going to go?"

I told the editorial board—at the *Post*, the *Times*, and the *Examiner*—we're going to trip and fall. We've not hit bottom yet. We're going to bring in the experts and move forward. I said in my first week to the board, I am going to try and close the gap from the deficit of $164 million and not have a fare increase this year. I closed it. We used money from the legal settlement and from other accounts, put it together, and reduced the administrative staff. We needed to show the public that we can be efficient.

Let me go back to the media and the agenda for a moment. The *Post* will cover everything that we do. My instruction to media relations is that if something negative happens, call them. You call them before they call you. I want them to know that we won't hide anything. At the same time, we're not going to accept an infringement on employees' character; we're not going to participate in that. We'll give you the positions, but we're not going to give you names. I have a good relationship with the media. My record with them is honest and straightforward. I will admit when we mess up, and I'll tell them what we're going to do. I make a commitment to them.

Dukakis—The press in this town appears to be focused on certain aspects of the operation. Editorially, do they have a vision, or are they focused on the details of operations?

Catoe—They've done both. On the vision side, we've talked about how important transportation and the Metro are to the region. To support that, we need dedicated funding. They've editorialized in favor of that. On the operation side, for example, there was an editorial on Thursday that dealt with operator overtime. I talked to the editorial writer for fifteen minutes about his editorial that was very critical of the agency. I told him what we're going to do. They printed that, with the comment "Good luck" and "You've got your job cut out for you."

Are they being fair to Metro? Well, we did some things that deserved negative press. When people are killed, until you fix it, everything that happens, they will hit you on it.

Dukakis—How did you deal with that overtime issue? Do you know why it's happening?

Catoe—Yes. One reason is that a few years ago the board did not want to see an increase in headcounts. So as we expanded services, we didn't increase the number of mechanics and drivers. Back-up drivers were used, and when someone was absent, everybody worked overtime. We're going to put sixty more drivers in the system to cover this situation. These additional hires will cost more. So I am managing that.

The other issue is the culture. I found this out by walking around and talking to station managers. These people are usually in the kiosk office areas. I would see this one guy every day, including weekends. I said, "Bill, you sure work a lot." He responded, "I'm nearing retirement, and my manager, since I have been a good employee, lets me work all the overtime I want." The reason for this is because retirement is calculated on the highest four years of wages. Here, management is doing this. They have no connection to the financial aspects of the organization. They've not been told, trained, or held accountable. This is the culture. Bill is a good guy. But this is changing.

Dukakis—You've talked about this as well, but in terms of implementing your goals, what's the key to making that happen? I assume people are a part of it.

Catoe—All of it. We need to get the right people in place. And we need to get them to change their behaviors. Less than half of the executive team is people who were here before. Dick Wright, who was the general manager, did not watch the system in the last six months. He was being told that everything is wonderful. He didn't know any better; he didn't ride the system. I ride it every day.

When I arrived, I told my executive team, "You're going to ride the system." I told them, "When you ride it this week, you're going to walk up to the first Metro employee you see and ask them how things are going?" We're doing that. Our legal counsel said, "They're not going to want us to do that. They're going to ask 'Who are these people?'" But that's what we're going to do.

At the next meeting, she said she was shocked when she talked to the employee. She said, "The person thanked me for speaking to him and appreciated that I was using the system. Then he proceeded to start telling me stuff." That's now becoming a natural part of the executive team. At every meeting, members of the team report on what they learned while riding the system. That's going to become part of their direct reports. Pretty soon it starts spreading in the organization.

Dukakis—Did you use that approach in your previous jobs as well?

Catoe—I've done it before, but I'm doing it far more here. I need to. The culture here is more broken than at any agency I've been at before. By "broken" I mean that people are not proactive; they are reactive. The broken pipe case I used earlier is an example of this. This is a $2 billion agency, and we're critical to this region, and this utility hasn't called back? There is a lack of taking it to the next step. The response was "Oh well, I called, and they didn't return my call." It should be, you follow through until you get it done. That proactive approach is missing in the culture of the organization. We're going to have to reestablish that. You do that by giving rewards for when it happens. You demonstrate it personally. And you let people know when it's not happening.

If people make mistakes taking a risk to better the organization, I encourage them and I support them. I will cover for them from the standpoint that I will take any criticism for mistakes they made, as long as they were focused in the right way. But when we fail to act, I have no tolerance for that. That's unacceptable. I communicate that and I demonstrate that. If individuals do not learn from that, then the three-strike rule applies. I have the wrong person in the job.

Dukakis—Have there been important differences in the three organizations that you've worked at? Santa Monica is small and local. Los Angeles is quite large. Washington, DC, is really national. You've described Washington as broken and dysfunctional. Are you doing your job in about the same way as you did in the previous two?

Catoe—There are specific things I do that are different, but the issues are the same. In Santa Monica it was very small and local. You could talk to everyone because there was one location. I developed my skills, tested things, and found out what works. Part of it was natural. I really like people. I had truly bright people. I would talk to people about what worked and didn't work. It wasn't perfect. People make mistakes. I say "OK." If you really get people to focus, and they start getting praise, and they know they're the best, they are going to act like the best.

In Los Angeles, it was a much bigger organization. While transportation was not as important among many residents, it is increasingly becoming more important. It will be at the same level of importance as in Washington in the not too distant future. I worked to get people to understand how important the work is. At the same time, we had to be financially prudent with limited dollars. That was hard to do. In my first six months I felt overwhelmed. How am I going to get through this? It was difficult. I was talking to a group that was saying, "What language does he speak? We don't do things like that. That's not the culture of this organization."

It took a good five years in Los Angeles to get people to focus on how we structure the organization and how we become focused on our customers. Before, people said it doesn't make any difference what our customers do. That's wrong. That's not what we're here for. We're here to move them in a way they are satisfied. The whole image of the organization began to change. I believe that with the leadership they have in certain jobs, they are going to leap forward.

Coming here, this is an even bigger nut to crack. From an infrastructure standpoint, the system has been neglected. What is happening is true in this industry in a lot of locations. There was too much focus on expanding the system. There were operating facilities that were a hundred years old; bathrooms in employee facilities that hadn't been worked on in fifty years. What does that say to your employees? We're focusing on that. We're fixing those things. We can't do them all at once, but people know we're working on it.

But every place that I've gone in maintenance in the rail area, I've told employees that I'm embarrassed. Every day that I step out in the system, I feel embarrassed that we're putting these cars out there. They say, "But we can't fix that." No, we're going to fix it. They know personally where I'm coming from about this system. Most people don't want the general manager to be embarrassed. They look at it differently now. They're looking at the cars and seeing that they are dirty. They're the ones who will have to come up with the solution.

The difference here is international in scope. Coming back here was not just about the money. In the first month, I would wake up in my condominium and look out the window and say, "What in the hell am I doing here? Why did I do this?" I could have stayed in LA and been a consultant. I came here because I love to fix stuff. My success is that when I leave, this system is far better than what it is now.

We can get to the number one rating. In real terms, it's going to be one and a half to five years. It will be ingrained at that point. I'll be here to make that happen. I've trapped myself in, which you have to do. There will be good people and good managers in place. There will be good managers who are going to keep it that way. Then I'm happy. I'm ready to step away and say, "Now, here it is." And then let people run the system. I don't need my name on the wall anywhere or pictures of me hanging in buildings.

I enjoy sitting back and watching people be great. It's like a teacher who sees his students go off and succeed. The students may not ever send a note, but you can see that you were involved in having that happen. That needs to happen here. When I leave, I want this to be a great organization. That's the reward I want. That's what I will feel good about.

Thomas W. Payzant

Former Superintendent, Boston Public Schools
Interviewed by Michael Dukakis and John Portz
June 5, 2007
Cambridge, Massachusetts

Portz—Thanks for taking the time for this interview. In our project, one of the issues we are looking at is the relationship between leadership and management in the public sector. Are they different? Are they similar?

Payzant—I think there is a continuum. On one side of the continuum is leadership and on the other side is management. The two converge in the middle. Sometimes you function more in management, and sometimes you function more as a leader. At some point I think there is a lot of ambiguity about trying to make fine distinctions. I think of management more as learning a set of skills that focus on the work of technical change, improvement, and operations. Relationships and people skills are important, but not to the same extent as I think they are in leadership where leaders must set the vision, core values, and strategies for the adaptive changes necessary to achieve desired results.

I think at some point you're doing both. We've come to talk about leadership style and management style as though it was like putting on a new set of clothes. What I've come to realize over the years is that you can learn to modify certain aspects of the way you behave which may be categorized as style. However, knowing who you are and behaving in a way that is consistent with what you say are really important. My mother used to remind me that the connection between what people say and what they do helps you to learn a lot about them and whether or not you can trust and admire them. Sometimes there is a disconnect between those two. I think that really is what leadership and management are all about in terms of the way the work is done, results are achieved, and accountability is embraced.

I think leaders do need a vision about where they want to take an organization and how they're going to get it there. A manager can be in a situation where he or she inherits somebody else's vision and somebody else's constituted plan. A manager needs to buy into this and also needs the skills to get people

119

together to do the work. A manager needs some on-the-ground kinds of skills to work with people to make it happen. I think there is a higher expectation for a leader, given that there are managers at all levels in an organization.

With respect to the substance of what one works on as a leader or manager, I have an open question in my mind and I'm really ambivalent with regards to the question "Do you have to know the work to lead the work?" I was a nontraditional superintendent from the standard or perspective of the 1960s when I started in education. I began my first superintendency when I was not quite twenty-nine. I had not sat in all the chairs or experienced a variety of leadership roles. I had come back to Harvard to earn my doctorate after two years of teaching in an inner-city junior high school. I served as administrative assistant to the superintendent in the New Orleans public schools from 1967 to 1969. Then, a liberal board in a suburban Philadelphia school district wanted to do something dramatic after their superintendent retired who had been there for twenty-five years. Thanks to the support from one of my professors at the Harvard Graduate School of Education who helped school districts find superintendents, I was granted an interview. Much to my surprise, I was offered the position even though I had never served as an assistant principal, principal, central office line administrator, or assistant superintendent.

I struggle with this issue. I look at nontraditional superintendents today with this issue in mind. I'm doing executive coaching with people who come out of the Broad Academy [organization that trains non-educators to be superintendents]. I sometimes joke with the press about this, commenting that nobody's invited me to apply for a CEO position in a Fortune 500 company. Do you really have to know the work? If you're in the service industries, can you go to manufacturing? If you're in manufacturing, can you go to high tech? When I read *Good to Great* [a study of leadership in eleven successful companies, by Jim Collins], I was very surprised at the end of the book. Of the ten or eleven people that Collins was writing about, all but one of them had come up through the organization to become CEO. So I'm still struggling with this question. What it takes as a nontraditional leader is to have a very clear understanding of your strengths and weaknesses and the skill to assemble an executive team with the necessary skills to bump the balance necessary for any high-functioning leadership team.

Dukakis—Where do you come out on that question with respect to education?

Payzant—All things being equal, I think in this day and age management is not good enough. There's got to be leadership from the principal and from the superintendent, and you have to know something about teaching and learning. The name of the game is how you get other people to shoot for high standards and improve the quality of instruction in the schools to raise achievement for all kids. You either have to know something about that or be a very quick learner and surround yourself with several people who are real experts in the field.

I rambled a bit, but I wanted to provide some context in terms of my thinking and what I'm wrestling with. I've learned a lot over the last forty years about teaching and learning, but I don't consider myself a real expert. I know a little about a lot of things, and I can go deep in some areas, but I don't think I'm an expert across the broad field of teaching and learning. But I think a leader has to know something about the work. Not necessarily a deep understanding about the work, but to learn and understand what it takes to get the work done. The leadership challenges are particularly great in large urban school districts where it will take systemic thinking and strategies to improve whole systems of schools and not being content with the improvement of a few more schools.

Portz—But certainly within the education field you are perceived as someone who is traditional. Although you didn't go through the ranks in the standard model, you are well versed in the field.

Payzant—My point is that thirty-five years ago people looked at me and said he hasn't even been a principal. How can he supervise a principal and others in the school district who are older and have much more experience than he does? What I did have is two years of learning and doing in a major urban school district with a superintendent who was a great role model and mentor. I knew from that experience that I wanted to be a leader in urban education.

Dukakis—Did Roy Romer as superintendent in Los Angeles cross that threshold in terms of knowing the work?

Payzant—As governor of Colorado he had spent a lot of time on this issue and in the education field. He was known as one of the first education governors and he was eager to learn from the best leaders and policy-makers in public education. After he became superintendent in Los Angeles, he said it was the toughest job he had ever done, much more difficult than being governor.

Portz—When we think about the continuum you referred to earlier, and we talk about the skills of managers and leaders, did you find yourself operating more on the management side or the leadership side, or going back and forth between?

Payzant—I think back and forth. Part of it is that the culture in education is a tough one. Prior to the work of the last decade or so with a ratcheting-up of accountability, the philosophy was to hire the best people you can, put them in the classroom, and close the door and they'll do the best they can with the students they have. So, unlike other professions where there was much more collaboration and a willingness to learn from colleagues and take constructive criticism, the dominant school culture discouraged collaborative learning and believed that suggestions for improvement were often unfair and undeserved. I got better at leading and managing in this environment over the years. I don't think most leaders and managers like to make the tough personnel decisions, but that is the guts of the work, particularly in a school or school district where 80 percent of your budget is in people and we know that the quality of instruction in the classroom is the most important variable which the school controls for improving student learning, and the leadership of principals is second.

Dukakis—In Boston you had a chief operating officer to assist you as a leader and manager. Did you always have a chief operating officer, a number two, or was that a new direction in Boston?

Payzant—It was the first time that I had used that title. In Boston, I had both a chief financial officer and chief operating officer. In San Diego, I had a chief financial officer and then there was a business manager who at one point oversaw a variety of service areas, including transportation and food services and all the other operations side of the house, except finance. I had different approaches in different districts, such as a deputy superintendent for teaching and learning in Boston. In developing an organization, we often start in the pure sense of having the organization the way we would like it, but then there is the reality of who fills the position on the chart. Sometimes I have had to alter the organizational chart and reporting lines to get the right fit. You can create the most beautiful organizational design, but if you don't have the right people with the necessary skills in the right places, the organization won't work.

I believe the most important decision in designing a school system is to determine who will be responsible for selecting, supervising, and evaluating the principals. They are, as I said, the most important leaders in a school district except for the superintendent. School principals have to understand a lot more about what goes on in classrooms and how to observe and evaluate teachers. They need to lead the professional development work, and that's not just a checklist for management. It really requires them to lead the conversations about education, teaching, and learning, getting people fired up about the importance of their work, and not allowing people to say, "If the parents would just send us better kids, we could teach them better." It takes leadership and management too. We must focus on instructional leadership and how to inspire and support the teachers whose instruction must continue to improve to make a positive difference in student achievement.

However, school leaders still have to be able to make good hiring and separation decisions, develop strategic plans, use data for decision-making, balance budgets, embrace accountability, and engage parents and the community. They have to be able to develop the budget and work within available resources, which requires good management skills. As a leader you must help followers embrace your core values and vision. Good managers do that too, but there are a lot of situations where management decisions have to be made to enable the school district or schools to succeed even though they may be controversial (e.g., budget cuts, downsizing, or closing schools).

Portz—What have been your major strengths as a superintendent? You've been quite successful in a number of places. What would you attribute that success to?

Payzant—I would start with governance. There aren't too many superintendents that have had the same experience that I have with a long run in two large urban school districts—ten years and eight months in San Diego, and ten years and nine months in Boston. With respect to governance, San Diego was an elected board with five members. They ran, and still do, from five districts. Then, the two top vote-getters in each district in the primary election run in the general election on a citywide ballot. It's not just single member districts; they must run citywide, but they come from the district. That board didn't turn over completely until I had been there six or seven years. The only time there were open seats was when an incumbent decided not to run again. Usually, this change happened one seat at a time. So there was real continuity of leadership on the board and a commitment to continue effective policies.

I think continuity in leadership, whatever the governance structure, is critical if an organization is going to be able to get the right balance between sustainability and change. There are important core beliefs and values in the district, which drive the priorities and the work that must be done. If there is a lot of churn on the board side, there is usually churn on the executive side as well because the first thing a board can do when there is a new majority is get a new superintendent. It is the continuity in leadership on the governance side that can lead to continuity in leadership on the executive side. When they come together on what the goals are going to be, and they stick with them over time and don't have a new agenda every year, that is fundamentally what it is going to take to get the kinds of improvements that are badly needed. It is impossible to establish systematic reforms and get significant improvement in student achievement in just two or three years.

So if you're a teacher out in the schools, or a principal out in the schools, and you're in a district where the superintendents are turning over and maybe the board as well, every time there's a new board majority and it wants to put its stamp on the system, there's churn. There's rarely a conversation about sustainability and change, and what policies and practices should be continued, and what the issues are that will require change, whether moderate or radical, to move the district forward.

It is critical to get clarity around a few key goals, stick with them, and have a plan for doing work that will be coherent. Superintendents have to be constantly helping boards understand what is required so that the people who are doing the work in schools understand the connections between their work and the board's goals. They need to understand that professional development and improving instruction are part of everybody's responsibility and not something that someone else does. It's important to bring together teachers in instructional leadership teams and provide opportunities for teachers to develop some leadership and ownership of the school's improvement plan. It should not be just the principal who owns the plan, but all the teachers and staff in the school. Sometimes people talk about projects, but that's not what we should be talking about. We need to focus on those activities where we have some evidence that they will impact critical variables that make a difference in teaching and learning.

The second major point is the movement to standards-based reform and the commitment we are making to enable *all* students to achieve at the level we historically expected only select groups to reach. We need to think much more systemically about the work. I hadn't thought about it quite as clearly before coming to Boston. It was a matter of looking at a system of schools rather than individual schools. That is a different kind of thinking on the part of the board and superintendent.

Portz—School superintendents, and leaders in general, often confront many day-to-day issues that lead them to lose their focus. They end up bouncing from one crisis to the next. How were you able to avoid that? Did you do better in this area in Boston than in San Diego or other places where you've been a superintendent?

Payzant—Yes, perhaps. Boston *is* different. I knew that coming into Boston this would be my last superintendency. And I had never been offered a five-year contract in my entire career. Boston was very clear that it wanted a five-year commitment. I had never had more than a three-year contract. That was unusual. Also, having grown up here and having watched the city from a distance since I left in 1967, I knew something about the politics in Boston. People are sometimes surprised when I say that even though San Diego is more than twice the size of Boston, Boston is three times more complex than San Diego. So I was worried about keeping focus here.

The only way I could really offset that was to have a plan that was tight, focused, and relentless. There were going to be lots of distractions; I knew that. The ongoing concerns about student assignment would consume me. About every three years that I was here I spent an incredible amount of time on that issue. When I began my work here, the federal court case challenging the set-aside for black and Latino students issued by Judge [W. Arthur] Garrity during the 1970s ensuring a fixed number of seats for them at Boston Latin School had just been filed. The case took a lot of time my first year, followed by the Weisman case [student assignment court case] that came after that, and then several years later there was another case about student assignment. Then, just in the last two years, there's been another round of issues over student assignment.

During the most recent review we held more than twenty community forums. What we heard was clear. Parents want to be guaranteed access to their neighborhood schools, if that's where they want their children to go. Parents that don't want their neighborhood schools want other options. It's pretty hard when you have a lot of evidence from neighborhood meetings across the city and from a task force assigned to look at this issue that the community at large is split on the issue. We made a number of changes, such as changing the assignment algorithm, but basically we stuck with our policy of having a balance between the seats allotted for walk-zone students and for those outside the walk zone of each elementary, K–8, and middle school. At the high school level there is citywide choice. The demographics have changed dramatically.

And the other big challenge that diminishes somewhat with each passing year is the issue of race. There are whites and blacks who look through the lens of race and haven't recognized the changes that are apparent today. Also, there have been important shifts in the diversity within the Asian, black, and Hispanic racial groups, as well as within different language groups. It has changed the dynamic dramatically.

Dukakis—On your point of governance, if you had a choice, would you rather report to a mayor or to a school board?

Payzant—I have worked with elected school boards in four different districts in four different states and regions of the country and with an appointed school committee in Boston. In San Diego, there was continuity of leadership sustained through my tenure there with an elected board. In Boston it was also the case because of the continuity of leadership the mayor provided with the appointed school committees and their commitment to improve the Boston public schools. It's a question of time and relationships. I spent three to four times as much time with the board in San Diego as I did with the school committee here in Boston. However, if you added time spent with the mayor and the city council, along with the appointed school committee, the commitment is more substantial. Again, it all comes back to the relationships and understanding of roles and responsibilities.

If there is an issue with a lot of public testimony at a school committee meeting, a meeting that typically took two hours would run longer. Executive sessions were very short, because the only issues discussed were legal issues and collective bargaining. One of the best things that ever happened in the 1993 Massachusetts education reform law was when superintendents were given control over personnel, and principals were taken out of collective bargaining. If principals had stayed in collective bargaining here, I would not have been able to lead the district with a major commitment to develop and appoint principals who could lead instrumental improvement and raise achievement.

Timing also was important. If I had come to Boston earlier in my career, I probably would not have been good for Boston. I would have had more ego in the game. Coming here when I did, I didn't care who took credit for what. I had a national reputation, and I didn't expect a lot of recognition, as long as I could get the support I needed to get the job done.

I had a great relationship with the mayor. Mayor [Thomas M.] Menino and I are very different in many ways, but we shared common goals and developed deep respect for the roles and responsibilities we each had. We knew we needed each other at a very pragmatic level. We liked each other. The continuity of leadership on the school committee was very important. Liz Reilinger served as chair for most of my tenure.

But the city council was like having another school board, reviewing budgets and other aspects of the schools. With respect to the council, Mike Contompasis, my chief operating officer for a number of years, was a great help. We developed a great partnership. For most of our tenure there were anywhere between three and five members of the city council who came from Boston Latin, where Contompasis has been headmaster. To these councilors, Mike was still the headmaster. We did a "good cop–bad cop" routine. It made it a lot easier.

Portz—Where does the vision come from that you've referred to several times? How is that developed?

Payzant—I think the core values were with me when I started teaching. Early on, I wouldn't have gotten into this work at all if it wasn't focused on kids. And then the experience in New Orleans pushed me even further. Even before standards-based reform made it clear that education was for all kids, I would go back to the strong voice of public education and its importance to serve the common good in our democracy. Public education is what should enable all students to access opportunity. It's the American story. We've had some bad chapters with pervasive achievement gaps, and we're still not where we need to be, but that, basically, has been what's driven me throughout my career to try and move us closer to the ideal.

Having had the experience here as a northern liberal and then going into New Orleans in the late 1960s, I got hooked on urban education. I also taught in an inner-city junior high school in Tacoma, Washington. It was the best thing that could have happened to me. The school district had promised me a high school teaching job before I went there, but when I arrived, they said it was not available. However, they said they had a good deal for me, teaching four classes in a junior high school and working in the lunchroom every day. I was twenty-two years old and teaching ninth graders. It was that experience, plus the New Orleans experience, that led me to know that I wanted to make a positive difference in urban education. It was all driven by the value that our focus needed to be on providing opportunities for all students to succeed. That's the American dream. That's public education. That's why it is so important for us not to lose sight of the common-good argument.

I'll tell you a story that I think you can resonate with. In the summer of 1952, my parents bought a black-and-white television. I cut lawns and did a few other things, but there wasn't much else for me to do. I watched both the Democratic and Republican party conventions; I was fascinated by them. The conventions were mainly about the platform. The front end of the convention was about what was going to be in the platform. Then the delegates would decide who was going to be the nominee for president. The nominee would take the platform, and that was what the campaign would be all about—selling the American people on the platform, which was the plan for addressing all of the central issues the country faced.

In contrast, my whole career has covered the years marked by the rise of special-interest politics. It is much easier to see the alignment on the issues and have coherence in a platform. Part of the challenge with respect to leadership is dealing with this new special-interest environment with single-issue advocates demanding adherence to their views as the condition for a candidate receiving support. Elected officials are under tremendous pressure to make a nod to just about every special interest. Today, we have presidential candidates making lightning shifts on core value issues. You couldn't do that back in 1952 and get away with it. The party platform was the North Star. The whole was greater than the sum of its parts and clarified the difference between the policy directions Republicans and Democrats would take to keep America strong.

I'm doing some coaching work with school leaders in several different districts. Class issues are often present. I'm working with a superintendent in Aurora, Colorado. It's a classic district where the old Aurora that borders Denver is low-income, while near the prairie there are new 3,000- and 4,000-square-foot homes for middle- and upper-income families. Parents want money for their students in their neighborhood. They ask, "Why are you spending money on those kids?" Equity issues are tremendous. I think that people in leadership positions in urban school districts have to really put the equity issue on the table. Equal expenditures per student falls short of what is needed to address equity challenges where some students will require additional support to give them a chance to succeed.

Portz—In your coaching work with superintendents, do you ask the question to yourself "Does this person have core values?"

Payzant—Yes. We actually talk about it. Core values underlie a theory of action. Ten years ago I didn't even know the term "theory of action." I don't think it was around in the early 1990s, but since then, leaders are expected to have a theory of action. When you come into a new organization as a leader, you've got core values and perhaps some goals, but what you need is a theory of how you're going to reach those goals and stay true to your core values. So at a very simple level, my theory of action, although I didn't call it that for a long, long time, has been—it's all about the people and the quality of instruction in the classroom. And I think the way I sharpened it in Boston relates to my focus on leadership development in principals.

My theory of action is a laser-like focus on teaching and learning in the classroom and what you do to support teachers to get better at what they are doing. Importantly, you have to get the right people in the principalship to lead the work. That's basically how I've thought about it during the last decade. I've learned more at each stage of my career from what has worked and mistakes I have made. I think I'm a little more sophisticated about what it takes to do the work and able through my coaching of first-time urban superintendents and teaching aspiring school and districts leaders how to avoid some of the mistakes I've made and learn from what has worked for me as a leader.

The other thing I have learned is that the context for student learning is going to be in some ways similar and in some ways different in different schools and classrooms. But your core values should carry over from district to district. Then the challenge becomes, where the context is different, to maintain the core values and have them be enabling in terms of the work. There are certain generic things I have found in the places I've been a superintendent, but Boston has some very unique features, some of which go back to the desegregation experiences of the 1970s. You have to build that in, at least in terms of strategies of how you're going to do the work. I knew that, but I learned a lot more about it, once I was here. As a former history teacher I know that we must learn about the past as a way to avoid mistakes that were made and also respect actions that were taken to better shape the pursuit.

Portz—In talking about the importance of context in leadership, let's shift for a moment and turn to your experience in the federal government. It was much shorter than your superintendencies. How did that different context impact your ability to be a leader?

Payzant—I actually intended to be in Washington as assistant secretary for elementary and secondary education for four years. I kept saying "no, no, no" to the Boston search; I was lobbied very hard to throw my hat into the ring. I talked to Secretary of Education Dick Riley and Senator Ted Kennedy and others about the position. It was not my plan to leave at that time, but they supported me when I applied for the Boston superintendency.

I was in Washington at a very interesting time. I had the opportunity to work on Goals 2000, a major piece of legislation. I learned a lot that later benefited my work in Boston. It was a different environment. When the White House called, or when Secretary Riley called, I responded immediately. I had never left so many people in the waiting room as I did in Washington. I would go to so many events—endless events—but I got used to that whole culture. This was new to me. I had worked with state legislatures in the past, but this was different. Some questioned whether I could get the job done; they would say, "He doesn't know how to work inside the Beltway." I did a lot of testifying on Capitol Hill. I had been working with school boards and state legislatures for a long time. What's so different about this big legislature on the hill? I actually did fine. I was honest with them. If I didn't know something, I would say, "You'll have the information tomorrow." And I wouldn't give them convoluted, long answers to their questions. In addition, I had a good relationship with the staffers. There were not many practitioners in leadership positions, and the members of Congress responded positively to candid answers about how policy proposals would affect educators and students in school districts and schools.

I remember going to the office the first day at 7:00 a.m. and nobody was there. Then I finally got into the Washington rhythm and I went to work at

8:00 or 8:30 and would work until 8:00 or 8:30 at night, particularly when I was working on legislation or getting ready to testify. Also, I was on the road a lot, making speeches and representing the administration. I didn't work most weekends, except when we were filing legislation or meeting some other deadlines. My wife and I had a great time in Washington. Most weeks I would at least get Sunday off unless I was traveling.

By comparison, being superintendent of schools in Boston is a 24/7 commitment. I set aside three weeks every summer for a family trip to Oregon. I didn't want any calls. I only had one crisis when I was gone. Some city councilors raised some issues and we talked over the phone. Chuck Turner [Boston city councilor] and a few others occupied an area near my office. He said we would have to get the police to pull him out of there. I talked to Chuck, saying, "Chuck, you and I are contemporaries. We remember the civil rights era of the 1960s; we were part of that. Do you think I'm stupid enough to have you removed? . . . See you Sunday when I come back to town." He stayed. When I came back, the mayor said to me, "You handled the situation pretty well, but you made one mistake: you didn't lock the bathrooms."

But to return to my Washington experience, I spent about one-third of my time on the road, one-third or a little better on Capitol Hill, and one-third trying to manage the Office of Elementary and Secondary Education in the Department of Education, which had about 300 employees. This management responsibility was one of the most challenging experiences I've had. The office had political appointees, senior career civil service, mid-level career people, and then all of the clerical, custodial, and support folks. Most of the secretaries and clerical staff, which were the low-paying jobs, were black. Far fewer of the career employees in the professional positions were people of color. There was a lot of action around the race issue. Part of the dynamic was that there was a liberal, Democratic administration and a lot of pent-up frustration left over from the Republican administration by people who had few opportunities for advancement. I had to deal with the carryover of those resenting the lack of opportunities to advance to higher-level jobs and pay grades they experienced in the previous administration. That was a real management challenge.

There's always tension between political appointees and career people. You have to work with both sides. We did a lot of work on drafting legislation in which there would be real debates, particularly with career folks. They were fantastic; you couldn't do the work without them.

Also, I brought Janice Jackson in as my deputy. She had been an intern with me in San Diego. She provided a lot of support and helped to work various issues through the office culture. As a black woman, she and I had many conversations that helped me, as a white male, move issues forward.

Portz—Whether at the federal or school district level, a challenge for leader-managers is building coalitions. What seemed to work, and what didn't work, with respect to building coalitions?

Payzant—For school districts, I come back to the earlier comments about the complexity of an urban setting. I have been involved in a lot of work trying to develop ways to coordinate health, social services, and other supports for urban and often low-income families. However, it is very complex with many actors. In Boston, for example, there are dozens of leaders in health services, and it was always a challenge to decide who the key players were and to get them in a room to have the conversation of how to coordinate services. There are so many different players. It's a challenge to get people to come together and focus around a common agenda.

I was more successful in some areas than others. Part of the problem was time: how much I could do myself. Staff members in various organizations could get the conversation started, but unless agency leaders were involved, not much progress was made. I also realized that some issues, like health insurance, were bigger than the schools.

In this context, I come back to one of the benefits of being a member of the Boston mayor's cabinet. For example, I did work with the public health commissioner, who was on the cabinet; that didn't require a lot of people in the room. The Police Department is another example. As department heads we would see each other once a week in the cabinet. It made communication easier. We would do programs together, and if it was big enough, we would seek the blessing from the mayor. This provided a structure for bringing people together that I didn't have in San Diego, but it was still complex.

My San Diego experience provides a different model. We took a geographic area with a feeder pattern of elementary, middle, and high schools and created a group of leaders of various agencies providing support to the families who lived in those areas and whose students attended the identified schools. Everybody at the table was from different sectors. We asked them to go back and look at this geographic area and what kind of money they were spending there. This was an area with a lot of low-income and immigrant families. They found an array of services—free lunch, housing, health—being offered in different places. We tried to create a one-stop shop for many of these activities. We had to bring different kinds of people together and cross-train them. It was tough to put together, but it was a great model and had some success.

However, how do you take it to scale? It took eighteen months to work out an agreement where the welfare system could release data on the kids in the schools in that geographic area so that we could eliminate another process for families and designate the students as eligible for free and reduced-price lunch. It's very difficult to put all of this together. At the state and federal policy levels there has not been a lot of success bringing that kind of cross-departmental effort together. In Boston, we've done some cross-department collaboration in a variety of areas, including with the Health Commission and the Department of Social Services with Harry Spence.

With funders' groups, I found when I came to Boston a lot of fragmentation and little systemic effort. I want to say this in a very respectful way, but if the real goal is to make a difference for kids, grants of $3,000 to $5,000 to $8,000 are not going to do it. We needed to bring significant resources forward, bring money together, and use it to help implement core strategies for the district. The Boston Plan for Excellence, with Ellen Guiney as director, was a great partner. Ellen came at about the same time that I did and shared this perspective. The two of us worked together in making the case to others. We actually turned down funding in some instances if it wasn't in line with our work. That was viewed as a radical step to take, but it was essential and part of a longer-range strategy.

With national funders we followed a similar strategy. In the first Annenberg grant, for example, we pushed for a different model. Their preferred strategy was for districts to pick a subset of schools and work with them. I didn't want to do that. I wanted to show that a systemic approach could work to improve a whole system of schools. They wanted $10 million as the local match. With the help of Bill Boyan, who at the time was a member of the senior executive team at John Hancock, we raised $15 million in a year to exceed our goal. Of the original nineteen Annenberg grantees, only three, including Boston, were invited for a second round of funding five years later. We were the only one that was approaching the work systemically.

Dukakis—How did you work with the teachers? For most of your time in Boston, it seemed that you had a pretty good relationship with the teachers, although recently there have been some disagreements on pilot schools [within-in-district charter-like schools]. How did you approach the relationship?

Payzant—I didn't have to face contract negotiations my first year; that was very helpful. The district had gone through a very tough negotiation process in 1994. There was a significant amount of money put on the table, and the pilot school agreement was also included. The first pilot school opened in September 1995; I arrived October 1.

Ironically, when I was here in graduate school, I did my qualifying paper on the politics of passing the Massachusetts public collective bargaining law. Little did I know then that I would spend thousands of hours over the next forty years on this issue. I developed significant cumulative bargaining experience in each of the five districts I served as a superintendent.

My approach has been based on the premise that any dispute that the district has is with the union and not with the teachers. I would talk about the union, not about teachers. I would talk about the union president, not about Ed Doherty [long-time president of the Boston Teachers Union (BTU)]. Ed Doherty was a veteran. I met him early in my tenure, and my approach to him, and his approach to me, was that regardless of what was going on, we continued to communicate and work together. We had breakfast on a regular basis. That does not mean that the tension in the relationship didn't escalate during times when a strike was likely and only avoided at the eleventh hour.

I learned in San Diego the value of one-on-one meetings with the union presidents, although quite by accident. In working with union leadership, I always looked for a consistency between what was said and the actions that followed. That consistency wasn't always there. I learned that little subtleties can make a difference. You need to pay attention to them. Ultimately, the contract will be settled, and there will be another contract. It's a cycle. It was important to depersonalize the process.

At the breakfasts, we didn't have a formal agenda. We talked about the pressures and issues we were facing in our respective roles. During times of negotiation, we were careful to recognize that what we talked about at the meetings didn't necessarily carry over to negotiations. We stopped short of trying to cut a deal over breakfast. The conversation was typically more exploratory, as in "what if" kinds of discussions. The stability with having Ed Doherty as president of the union was important; he was there for six or seven of my eleven years as superintendent.

Dukakis—You made it a practice of visiting schools. What did you do when you made those visits?

Payzant—Yes, I visited schools every year. In my last year in Boston, because of issues pulling me in different directions, I probably only went to forty or fifty schools, but prior to that, I would visit 60 to 70 percent of the schools each year. During my first year I visited each of the 125 schools.

The purpose of the visits changed overtime. On the first visit, I usually allotted about an hour for an elementary school visit and additional time for middle and high school visits. I wanted to let people know I was there, to say hello, and that I would be back. And, importantly, I wanted them to know that I cared about their work. For the first couple of weeks, I announced the visits. But shortly thereafter, I made it clear that my visits would be unannounced. That bothered some principals and teachers during my first years. But I continued the process because I didn't want special preparations made for my visits. I wanted to see what was going on under normal circumstances.

My activities evolved over time, to where I wanted to get deeper into the teaching and learning work. I would spend more time in a few classrooms. The principal would often come with me. That was fine. I wanted to see what they were seeing. It was important to work with principals to help them to understand what good instruction looked like.

Portz—What were your goals in visiting schools? What did you see coming out of those experiences? Why was that so important to you?

Payzant—It goes back to an issue I raised earlier—you have to know the work to lead the work. Part of knowing the work is seeing the work that is being done and that you think should be done. And what can you learn from what you see and hear. The "walking around" allows you to do that. It also challenges the traditional view that superintendents sit in their offices and don't really know what the real world of schools is like.

Also, it is about relationship-building. The superintendent, like any leader who is removed from day-to-day contact with the work, can develop a mystique that separates him or her from what is happening in schools where the teaching and the learning work is done. You can become a distant name and title at central offices like Court Street, or on the six o'clock news, or a story in the *Globe* or *Herald*. But if you visit the schools, I don't care how big the system is, the word does get around. I had a master key, so I didn't have to ring the bell. The whispers would start—"The superintendent is here." It amazed me during my school visits throughout my career how many teachers would say, "You are the first superintendent to come to my classroom."

I also had personal reasons. If I was tired and frustrated by tough issues at Court Street or city hall, I would go out to a school and I would get pumped up. It reenergized me. You have to seek the kids and see the people who are doing the work. One of the biggest challenges in urban America is creating a sense of hope that you can make a difference for children in an urban school system. There is so much negativity. However, the stories of the young people who despite tremendous odds show incredible resilience, perseverance, and do succeed is what gives me both hope and confidence that urban schools and districts are improving and must continue to do so.

Portz—Did you do this in San Diego, with twice as many schools?

Payzant—Yes. I've always done this. It's fuel for me, but it also is very useful to know about the work that is happening in the schools. I can get a good sense of a school's climate just by walking around and watching what they are doing. I'd ask students, "What are you doing today?" They would respond,

"I'm working on this. I've been in this small group today talking about this assignment." Or I would go into another classroom—"More worksheets." You have to talk to the kids.

Portz—Did these visits to schools have an impact on how you organized the district? You mentioned earlier the challenge of matching the right people with an organizational chart.

Payzant—Yes. In fact, one of my first decisions in Boston was to go back to the organization chart and have all of the principals report directly to me. That included 125 principals at the time. That was really ludicrous, but I did it for symbolic reasons, and it worked.

To get to this point, I actually used a political model. I created a transition team when I was hired. I was appointed in early August, but didn't start until September. I had Bob Peterkin from Harvard chair the transition team. I was coming up to Boston from Washington, DC, every weekend, and I would hear from this team. Part of the feedback was that there were too many layers. Janice Jackson came on board as my deputy in January. For the first year and a half, the principals reported to us. During this period, six principals were dismissed when their contracts ended. This had never been done. I expected resistance from the schools, but only one of the schools launched a campaign to keep their principal, which was not successful. The action I took was unprecedented and set the tone for a serious focus on school leadership.

That focus took the form of a leadership team and a cluster system. Since Boston didn't have feeder patterns, clusters were geographic, each with about twelve schools. The cluster leader, who was a principal at one of the twelve schools, was on my leadership team. Cluster leaders did not supervise their colleagues, but acted as conveners. I assigned the best principals to be cluster leaders. They were paid $1,000 a month to be conveners and sounding boards. Those ten cluster leaders were part of my senior leadership group; they were involved in decision-making. We met every two weeks for two hours. I was constantly sending the message that they were important and I wanted to know what was going on out in the schools and seek their guidance on district policy and budget issues.

Dukakis—What about rank-and-file teachers? How did you interact with them?

Payzant—I had contact with different teacher advisory groups, but I didn't have any regular way of seeing a particular group of teachers. Every year, except when we were fighting over a contract, the BTU would invite me to join them at their annual retreat weekend on a Saturday morning to meet with teachers. It was very important, even though I only did it once a year. Several times I went to membership meetings. The union president would tell me, "Come down and listen to the teachers. Hear what they are saying." I would. I also attended events in which teachers were present, and I attended many professional development programs. Every year I recorded an eight- to ten-minute video that was shown to all staff on the first day of school. I used this opportunity to set the tone and expectations for the year.

Dukakis—What about the media and general public relations? How do you work with the media?

Payzant—People are very surprised when I tell them that Boston is in the fifth-largest media market in the country. Leading a public institution may be similar in many ways to leading organizations in the private or nonprofit sectors. However, leading in the public fishbowl is different particularly because so much happens in public and even that which does not is subject to public scrutiny. Most states have statutory regulations that are based on open meeting laws. School boards make policy decisions in public. Most school districts' records are subject to public review.

In large urban school districts, few days pass without some type of media inquiry. I believe that one of the most important responsibilities of a leader is to develop policies and practices that address the many different aspects of systematic thinking about internal and external communications.

I have always believed the superintendent must be the lead advocate in the community for quality education for all children and must develop the skills necessary to use with different media. Some leaders see the press as their enemies. I see them as allies because the way leaders develop relationships with editorial boards, newspaper, radio, and television reporters can make a significance difference in what gets reported and how it is done.

I spent more time with the media in Boston than in any other superintendency. It was rare when I avoided taking a press call or avoided an interview unless I needed a little more time to be briefed on the issue I would be addressing. Press calls always had top priority on my return call list. I did not call reporters and complain about what they reported or conversely call with praise for a good article or television news piece. My communications people did that.

Leaders can never become satisfied that they are good enough as communicators. I continue to learn by watching and listening to others deal with interviews on radio and television, give prepared or extemporaneous speeches, function in settings with upset or angry people, craft their messages for internal documents, present reports and respond to questions at school board meetings and other public functions. These skills are important. I also believe that leaders must be forthcoming and admit mistakes when they make them and must understand that transparency in the public sector is very important in building credibility and support.

Federico Fabian Peña
**Former Mayor of Denver and Secretary of U.S. Departments
of Transportation and Energy
Interviewed by Michael Dukakis
July 18, 2009
Denver, Colorado**

Dukakis—Tell us a little about your early years in public service. You began your career as a lawyer?

Peña—Yes, I was a Reginald Smith Community Lawyer and I was assigned to a legal aid program in El Paso, Texas. I did that for about ten months and then moved to Denver, where I was a civil rights lawyer for a group called the Chicano Education Project. We represented Hispanic school children and Hispanic teachers here in Colorado. Later, I was involved in the *Keyes* case [U.S. Supreme Court case involving racial segregation in Denver schools] and a statewide school-finance case. I did that for two or three years.

Then, in 1978, I ran for the state legislature, served four years, and was minority leader of the House of Representatives during my second term. After two terms, I ran for mayor, won, and then served for eight years in that position. It was two four-year terms. In 1991, I started my own money management business called Peña Investment Advisors.

In late 1992, I was invited to help with the transition work for the Department of Transportation for President-elect Clinton. When I started the transition work, I walked into an empty office in Washington, DC. There was not a table or a paper clip. I had to assemble a team of sixty people from throughout the United States. From a list of about 400 people, I selected individuals who wanted to be a part of the transition team. We worked for about four weeks. We went into the Department of Transportation and evaluated all divisions. We went through every division and put together a fifty-page report for the president-elect. I submitted it on December 21 or 22 and left town because I figured Mr. Clinton was either going to pick Bill Daley [who became U.S. Secretary of Commerce from 1997 to 2000] or Governor James Blanchard of Michigan for Secretary of Transportation. Neither of them was selected, and they called me. I served as Secretary of Transportation for four years, and then I served at the Department of Energy for a year and a half.

I came back to Denver in 1998, and I've been a member of a private equity firm for the last ten years.

Dukakis—One question we're exploring is the similarities and differences between leadership and management. Are there two distinct sets of skills, or are they more similar?

Peña—My own judgment is that you have to have both sets of skills. Let me tell you my story. When I ran for mayor, I was seen as a visionary because my campaign slogan was "Imagine a Great City." I talked about all the great potential of the city and all that the city could become. People saw me as an idealist. In fact, some of my opponents labeled me "Freddy and the Dreamers."

I was running against an incumbent and six other candidates, and two of them were former cabinet members of Governor Dick Lamm. I was literally a dark horse, but I won. Within ten months of taking office, Denver went into one of the worst recessions in the history of the city. This was in 1983–84. Everything was affected. Energy was down, agriculture was down, housing was down. Everything imploded in this part of the country. The two coasts were doing fine. It was a bicoastal economy and we in the middle of the country were suffering. It was one of the worst recessions. Our unemployment rate was 2 percent above the national average. We had a vacancy rate in downtown office space of 30 percent. We had record foreclosures, record bankruptcies, and a net loss of population in the state of Colorado. This had never happened before. People were just leaving; they couldn't find work here.

I had to develop a strategy to claw our way out of this recession. That required management skills. We needed to build an airport. What was that going to cost? We needed to build a convention center. What would be that cost? We needed to rebuild viaducts and other infrastructure, which were falling apart. We had several viaducts that were rated 4 or 5 or 6 out of 100 on the national scale. These were dangerous viaducts. We had a lot of things that were deteriorating.

At the same time, I was a visionary, and I was a leader. People wanted to come to work for me. The same thing has happened with President Obama; everybody wanted to work for him. I was able to attract new blood, smart young people, and also mature, experienced people who had worked in state or city government. My leadership skills, having a vision, uplifting people, and giving people a sense of purpose and excitement generally came naturally.

Dukakis—And you did that as a legislator, too?

Peña—Somewhat, but it was different. We had to have an agenda, and I developed one as minority leader. The legislature was Republican, and the governor was a Democrat. But on the other hand, I had to have some management skills. And I developed those.

Dukakis—The city was in a major economic downturn?

Peña—Yes, when I took office we had a $35 million deficit. To balance the budget, I took ten-days' leave without pay. Cabinet members took seven days without pay. I talked to all of the city's employees; they took five days without pay. There were tough decisions. We had to cut.

Then we took whatever remaining revenues we had and focused them on growth and investment strategies to build our way out of the recession. In my office I had a big board that had every project on it with timetables. My staff used to laugh at me and say, "What are you doing?" And I would say, "Well, I want a report on where we are with the airport. I thought that by October we were going to get the EIS (environmental impact statement) done." They said, "What are you doing that for? You're not a manager." They would actually tell me that. They said, "Let your chief of staff do that." I said "No, no. I want to make sure this is getting done."

Dukakis—Were there other capital projects?

Peña—There were a number of projects. We built a brand-new convention center. We passed a $240 million bond issue. Back in those days that was a lot of money. We had to sell that and a property tax increase even when people's property values were going down right in the middle of a recession. We had to convince people, particularly senior citizens, to support that. This was very, very difficult. We revitalized many neighborhoods and built streetscapes. We transformed our major, downtown library, and we transformed lower downtown into a historic district that is now prime real estate.

Dukakis—The city looks terrific.

Peña—Thank you. It does look great. We put in a lot of infrastructure and the foundation for what's happened since.

Dukakis—In this recovery effort you managed many of these projects?

Peña—I had specific people running projects. My airport manager ran the airport—the fifth busiest airport in the United States—and also simultaneously built a new airport. Another person was in charge of the convention center. I had very specific teams of people managing these projects day to day, but at a macro level, I wanted to know where the projects were. Furthermore, we had to issue revenue bonds and general obligation bonds, etc., and some people were saying that I would bankrupt the city because I was going into too much debt.

I argued a fiscal perspective to the editorial boards. "Yes, our debt is going to go up, but these are long-term investments; all the notes are going to be paid back. Don't worry. And then the city will be stronger. Revenue is going to come back in because the economy is going to improve." That's exactly what happened. We never defaulted on a bond. People predicted the airport would go broke, but it's always done quite well. But it was challenging because people didn't see me as an economist; they didn't see me as a banker. And they said, "Why should we believe these investments are going to pay off?" Importantly, I surrounded myself with some very smart people with financial backgrounds.

Dukakis—Would you call yourself somebody who is organized?

Peña—Generally speaking, yes. In terms of my personal life, I'm fairly well organized. I have always been financially conservative. Even as a kid, I always saved money. I was very conservative, influenced by my father, who was a conservative businessman. That's the way I run my own personal affairs. In the legislature we had to do the same thing, maintaining a balanced budget and surplus.

Dukakis—You were a successful mayor. You spoke earlier of your vision. What were other ingredients to your success?

Peña—You have to have passion. That passion comes from one of two sources. Either you really believe in something and you want something to be done, or you're really angry about something and you want to change it or stop something bad from happening. My passion came from the first. I'm a doer. I like to get things done. That was my passion.

Another key factor is determination. I don't know how many times during the airport project people said, "Let's stop it. This is never going to get done." I said, "No. Let's stay focused." People were saying, "This guy's crazy." We're building a brand-new airport, but the airlines were not supporting it. We went out to the bond market with Goldman Sachs and other bankers and sold bonds without written airline agreements. People said, "It never has happened; it won't happen. Nobody will buy those bonds." They were sold in record time. Of course we had to pay higher interest—10 percent. There was some criticism of this higher rate, but the main criticism was, "You're not going to be able to sell them." And when they sold, people exclaimed, "Wow!" So determination is critical. You may have to make a few adjustments as you go, but don't give up.

I think the other ingredient is surrounding oneself with very smart, talented people. This process started even before the election. The nature of my campaign was grassroots-based, very optimistic, and youth-oriented; we attracted a lot of very talented professionals. I had to figure out a way to bring on board the right people. I wanted people who shared my values, and I wanted people who could work together. I didn't want prima donnas. They had to be people who acted like I acted. I'm a people person, and I try to keep my ego in check as much as possible, so I wanted people to reflect my views. I didn't want people who were going to be mistreating citizens, or people with a tough edge who were going to rub people the wrong way. I was an inclusive person. I believed in bringing people together. During my campaign, gays got involved; labor was involved; all kinds of people were working together who never did before. I wanted my team to have that philosophy; we had to bring everybody together and work as a team.

When it came to making appointments to boards or commissions, and there were many, we had many new individuals who wanted to get involved. I had a group of advisers who would help me screen candidates. I was looking for balance. I was looking for people from every walk of life. When I was running for mayor, I wanted the government to reflect the entire city as it had not previously. In fact, it had not for decades. It was essentially a white, male-dominated city government. I blew those walls apart and completely changed that practice. Some people were very uncomfortable with this change and were not sure a diverse government would work.

Dukakis—When you were picking your cabinet, what were you looking for?

Peña—Most of all, I wanted talented people. I wanted a team smarter than me. Some came out of government; some came out of the private sector. One person came out of labor. There were some people who came from the environmental community. So in a sense, at the end of the day, my team reflected all the various citizens who supported me in my campaign. So I had a lot of women, minorities, neighborhood activists, environmentalists, gays, and people with labor and business backgrounds.

Dukakis—Were all these people successful?

Peña—No. Some people did not work out. I think one of my faults was that I was not quick to replace people who did not work out. I had a tendency to give people a second chance or even a third chance. I didn't have extensive management experience. I think more experienced managers will tell you if you have someone who is not working out, you probably need to make a quick change. I sometimes kept people on for a little longer than I should have, and I finally had to terminate them. But by that time, it was a difficult and messy situation. So I looked for talent; I looked for diversity; I looked for people who reflected my philosophy.

In general, being mayor is not as much fun when you are in a major recession. There's nothing worse for a leader—a governor or a mayor—than a recession. It is painful because people are hurting. There's a lot of pressure. I was working seven days a week. I was out every night speaking to practically any group that wanted to hear from me. These were long hours and difficult, painful decisions.

In my first four years as mayor people were impatient and critical since a lot of my projects were long-term. I had a difficult time my second election. People asked, "Well, where's the airport? Where's the new convention center?" I said, "Things take time to build. They don't happen overnight." So another mistake I made was not having enough short-term projects so that people could see immediate progress. Not until my second term did citizens begin to see progress.

Dukakis—Then you moved to the federal level. How did being mayor prepare you for those jobs? How was it different?

Peña—At the national level I was in charge of the Department of Transportation with 110,000 employees and a $30 billion budget.

One key difference was that I made close to 100 appointments, but I couldn't put my team in place quickly because many appointees needed Senate confirmation. When I was mayor I had control over picking my team, but in Washington it took me months. It took me a whole year to have my full leadership team; that was challenging. In addition, when I was secretary of transportation, the president would in some cases send someone to me to appoint. And there were guidelines. He said, "When you make your appointments for this department, pick people from all over the country and think about the states where we did very well in the election."

Secondly, the difference at the federal level was that I had to answer to OMB (Office of Management and Budget) and to the White House. Denver doesn't have a city manager; it is a strong mayoral form of government. Of course, we had to negotiate at times with various people, but the mayor had a lot of power. In Washington, I had to shape my budget as part of the total government budget, and OMB had to make decisions about who was going to get what funding. And then the president decided that we were going to balance the budget and eliminate the deficit. As a result, I had to cut 10,000 people from my department in about three and a half years. And we did. Then we were left to work with whatever resources remained.

Another difference was that as mayor, I could see more quickly the results of our work. As secretary of transportation we were essentially putting money out and funding all kinds of projects. However, these would be built past my term. I couldn't see the results as quickly as I could when I was mayor. As mayor, I could see new streetscapes, parks, and recreation centers. You get immediate feedback, and you can see results from what you're doing. But in Washington, everything took so long. You didn't see the results as quickly; that was a little frustrating.

Also, you're more detached physically. As mayor, you're present and available. People would call you at home. Citizens would demonstrate in front of my house. But when you're in Washington, people don't do that. When you're in Washington, the perception is that you are unreachable. There's this distance separating what you do from the citizens you're touching.

Dukakis—Did you have an agreement with the White House on appointments?

Peña—Not really. Taking the position and moving to DC happened so quickly. I didn't negotiate anything. But the White House was very fair with me. I brought in Steve Kaplan, who was my general counsel as mayor and became the general counsel for DOT; there were several other former associates as well. The White House understood I needed to have people with whom I was familiar on my team.

Dukakis—Was Congress involved?

Peña—Yes. Members of Congress, particularly senators who were involved in my confirmation, would say, "I'd like you to hire my legislative aide." They would say, "You're really going to like this person." And of course I didn't even know the person. I really had to walk a line in cases that involved powerful members of the Senate or House. You would try to find room. They would call the White House and tell the president, "I want Peña to hire —." I'd get a call saying to look at a particular person. And so I did that. I brought some in. Fortunately, they were all talented, but they were people I didn't know. That was a new experience. I hadn't done that before.

Dukakis—What about the size of the bureaucracy? With 110,000 people, was it your experience that it moved slowly, unlike what happens when you're mayor of a big city? Was that a problem? How did you deal with that?

Peña—That was a bit of a problem. The DOT had ten divisions when I was secretary: highways, transit, rail, National Highway Traffic Safety Administration, maritime, statistics, Federal Aviation Administration, Coast Guard, etc. The Coast Guard and FAA were the two biggest divisions in terms of people. The FAA had approximately 40,000 employees and the Coast Guard had 45,000. That's almost 90,000 of the 110,000. In the Coast Guard we had a commandant who typically came up through the ranks. Although the president has flexibility in the appointment, everybody kind of knows who is going to be the next commandant. They were very talented people.

The FAA was different. In the FAA you would bring in your own administrator. I found that changing the culture in the FAA was very challenging. It took a long time, and I'm not sure that we were ever fully successful. The FAA had a reputation for a "tombstone mentality" in which they would wait until after an accident had happened before they would finally change safety standards. The National Transportation Safety Board was always pressuring the FAA, saying, "Why haven't you passed this rule?" And the FAA would say, "Well, we've only had two accidents, and it's going to cost industry too much. There's no sense of doing it." I was of the other view. I was always pushing the FAA, saying, "Let's move forward; let's require these safety rules." The problem was that in the recession of the early 1990s the airlines had lost $12 billion. It was challenging for the FAA as an institution to require bankrupt airlines to make $100 million investments for safety equipment.

Some departments were more responsive than others. The Coast Guard ran itself. I never had to worry much about the "Coasties." They were conducting interdiction of Haitians and of Cubans. I would go on the high seas with them and watch them save people. They were very professional and reminded me of local fire departments. People loved them. They're all about safety; they're all about saving lives. They were well managed, had intelligent leadership, and rarely had issues like some of the other military departments, which would get in trouble for gargantuan overexpenditures.

Dukakis—Did you have a vision for the Department of Transportation?

Peña—Yes. I had two visions for the department. One was to fully embrace intermodalism. I understood this at the local level. I saw what happens when you connect people and their movements. My macro push at DOT was to get all these divisions—federal highways, federal transit, etc.—to work together. For example, if we're investing in San Francisco or Oakland, we wanted to connect the seaport to the child-care center at the transit stop to neighborhood housing. This whole notion of intermodalism—connecting things and people—was very important to me, the country, and our economy. I tried to foster this concept throughout the department and communities across the country.

The second vision was to encourage people in the department to understand that we were in the people business. This vision came from my time as mayor. I knew what it was like as mayor when I would battle Washington. I felt that few were listening, and few understood the concerns of local citizens and the concerns of local elected officials. So when I was in Washington and as staff came in with a rule, regulation, or a program, the first question I would ask is, "At the end of the day, when you go home after writing documents and pushing paper, can you say to yourself that you've helped one person—just one person—somewhere in the country because of something you did today?" This changed the attitude of some people who had been there for a long time—who were writing regulations or reviewing proposals or awarding grants and all that—and who didn't really touch people. I kept saying to everyone, "I want you to feel like you're touching people. What you do is more than just spend money and make investments. You're dealing with people's lives."

Dukakis—Were you part of the reinvention project of Vice President Gore?

Peña—Yes. Reinvention was about two key goals. First, it was about bringing private sector practices to the government so that we could save money, be more efficient in what we did, and challenge ourselves to think outside the box. Second, it was an effort to break down the walls that existed among the federal departments and then within each department. The goal was to collaborate and work more closely together. If you wanted to recreate the federal government, you wouldn't have the structure that you have today. Those were the two key efforts led by the vice president. We were very much a part of that. We won a number of awards. We were trying to be much more efficient and thoughtful.

Dukakis—When you went out in the field, what did you do?

Peña—For one, I listened. I would talk to local elected officials, neighborhood groups, labor organizations, and others. I remember when labor leaders came into my office at DOT; they would look around and said, "We haven't been in here for eight years."

It was important to listen. I've been a good listener most of my life. In Washington, people you have to listen to are very sophisticated and all of a sudden you were hearing people talking about, "What's the impact on Russia?" or "What's the impact on this part of the country?" or "How's this going to impact this whole industry?" Everything had enormous impacts and was complicated; it was at a macro scale. You really had to think through policies and decisions very carefully. So you had to be a good listener to make sure you didn't miss something.

Getting out in the field was important for me and my staff. I wanted them to travel, get out of DC, and go talk to our constituents. Again, it was the whole notion of making the department a "people place." I felt that way from my experience as mayor. "Let's get out, let's touch people." That's what the president believed in anyway; he was a people person. Let's let the average person know that we belong to them. We need to listen to governors, mayors, and county commissioners and try to find a way to be part of their dreams.

I did something else kind of interesting. Once a month I would conduct a lottery lunch. Any person in the Department of Transportation could submit their name in a lottery to lunch with me. It was my way of reaching out. For the first time, people started talking to "The Secretary." I was on the seventh floor and insulated. People would see me and say, "We've never met a secretary before." This was so different than being mayor. As mayor, you're everywhere. Everybody knows you.

So we had a lottery where twenty people were chosen each month to have lunch with me. They would come in and bring their brown bags; I would have a brown sack myself. Anybody could be in the lottery. We'd close the doors, we'd have one staff person in the room, and then I would say to them, "You can ask me any question you want. Nothing you say will be used against you. So if you have criticism of something or somebody, you can tell me. If you have an idea or something you'd like to try, tell me. Any questions are appropriate." I had one staff person who would write down the ideas.

I learned a lot. Their questions covered almost everything. Some would focus on specific issues, like pay raises, or a grievance, or a complaint that someone hadn't heard from their supervisor in three months. And then someone would ask, "The president said last week that we were going to do this and do that. Were you in that cabinet meeting and what was the thinking there?" Some questions were very sophisticated. The range of questions was from top to bottom. Some would ask personal questions like, "How about your family? How are your kids doing?" I would answer the question. There were no rules. Not one.

I learned information that otherwise wouldn't come up normal channels. If I learned something disturbing, which I did every once in a while, I would sit down with the appropriate people in the department and address it, but confidentially.

Dukakis—Were folks frank with you?

Peña—Yes. I wanted them to feel comfortable. There was only one person from my staff in the room. I didn't want agency heads in the meeting. This was all off the record. I tried to make people comfortable. People said a lot of things about me when I was secretary of transportation. One of the things that I still hear today is that people liked me; people felt comfortable around me. They didn't feel as if I was this arrogant, aloof person from the seventh floor. They felt comfortable talking to me at those lunches. When I walked down the halls, people would say hello. I would pop into offices and say, "How are you doing?"

Dukakis—Was the Department of Energy different?

Peña—Yes. Energy was smaller in terms of the number of people who were actually at headquarters. But it was a pretty intense place. First of all, I wasn't confirmed for at least three or four months. And at Energy we had so many complicated problems. I was traveling all over the world, negotiating with the Russians, reviewing our nuclear weapons, and trying to clean up the nuclear sites where there were major contamination issues. For example, Rocky Flats here in Denver was finally closed. We cleaned up that site in record time. There were a lot of tense issues at that time.

Dukakis—In terms of your approach to the two departments, was that about the same?

Peña—Yes. It was the same philosophy, the same concept. One difference at Energy, though, was that many employees were scientists or engineers. They were highly technical people, probably more so than at DOT. Energy was formed out of the old Atomic Energy Commission. So I visited the labs and other nuclear production sites. I will never forget the first time I went to Los Alamos. I walked in there and was sent to a special room. They said, "We're going to share the story about how we created the atomic bomb."

One of my responsibilities was to deal with the reality that President Clinton had outlawed underground nuclear testing in Nevada. The government had previously conducted underground testing of new nuclear weapons as well as old nuclear weapons. Old weapons needed to be tested because they were stored and you wanted to make sure they weren't deteriorating. When we eliminated underground testing, we turned to computer simulations. Scientists would come in once a year, and we'd go through every nuclear weapon. I had to sign off that each one was safe. They'd sit down with me and go over the weapons: "This one's fine, check the wiring, and we had to replace this, but don't worry about that, we've got that covered." I had to verify all that and notify the president in writing that everything was working.

Dukakis—Tell me about the media and what role it played in your professional life. What skills did you develop to work with the media?

Peña—Working with the media was a real learning experience for me. When I was first in the legislature, the media didn't really follow me because I was the minority leader. It wasn't very intense. We had a media strategy that focused on getting the Democratic Party message out throughout the state. We obviously wanted to get more Democrats elected.

I really had a wake-up call when I was mayor. During the campaign there was a lot of media attention. It was more that media people were fascinated with my campaign, although they didn't think I was going to win. The night before the primary election, a reporter from the *Rocky Mountain News* called and asked, "How are you going to do tomorrow?" I said, "I think I'm going to come in first." He sort of laughed and said, "We think you're going to come in fifth." The media was way off base. They thought I was an interesting aberration.

Once I was elected and took office, I experienced an avalanche of media attention. People were excited. They were very moved by the election, by the campaign, by my team, and all that. I was somewhat unprepared for that. It was enormously intense. I had to watch everything I said and everything I did. It was hard. I learned that I had no background for that sort of focused attention and very little training, except for the campaign. But this was different than the campaign. This was very intense. Some of it was friendly, but some of it was not. To some media, I could say your shirt was red, and they would report that I said it was blue.

At first, I was very naive about the media. I had this notion that they would just naturally like me. I was a "good guy." Why would anybody not like me? I won the election. I had to learn the hard way. Media people would write articles after an interview, and I'd say, "That's interesting, that's not the interview I had." Professionals came in and started training me on how to deal with the media. They would say, "With this reporter, you have to be careful."

My chief of staff knew quickly that I needed media help. With interviews, I needed to learn how to answer questions, to not deviate and roam, which we're all prone to do. But also there was the notion of looking at an interview as a chess game. The only way to judge if you were successful was when you made certain points. If you don't say those things, you failed. I'd never heard that before. I had to learn that.

It was very helpful for me to develop a personal relationship with reporters. First of all, I wanted the media to know that I would be truthful with them. They never had to worry about whether I was telling them the truth. I would never lie to the media. Developing that sense of trust was very important.

Secondly, I think towards the end of my public career, they started to realize I was actually halfway intelligent. Once, when we held a press conference in the mayor's office, one media person—I won't mention his name—made a racial comment about me. I didn't hear it. Another media person overheard it and called my chief of staff after the meeting and said, "Do you know that so and so said this about the mayor." The comment was about my ethnic background. He called the head of the radio station that employed this reporter, and the guy was moved to a different assignment. So developing a personal relationship with the media was very important. They needed to know that some preconceived notion they had of me could be wrong and that I needed a chance to correct it.

Dukakis—As mayor, did you have a planned media strategy? And to what extent were you involved?

Peña—Yes, we had a strategy. I didn't spend a lot of time planning that out. I left that to my chief of staff and media director, who would say, "Look, I think this week we really ought to be talking about the environment. Let's do three environmental events or announcements." They did that kind of thinking, but I collaborated with them. They'd present the plan. They'd say, "This month we're going to do this, next month we're going to do this, and in six months we're going to have the groundbreaking for the airport, so let's put that out there." We'd do that kind of strategizing. That was also new to me; I had never done that as a legislator.

Dukakis—How was it different when you moved to Washington?

Peña—Basically, I was ready. There's nothing that prepares you better than serving at the local level where you're pounded every day. I had some tough media times here in the city when I was mayor. My honeymoon lasted a good ten months. But then it was over.

So I was ready for the national media. Also, many of the reporters in the national media had been reporting on departmental issues for a long time. Many were specialists. They knew a lot. They knew right away if you didn't know something or if you were telling them something that was incorrect.

But I found that they [national media] were usually more balanced than the local media in Denver. When I was mayor, we had two newspapers that were very competitive. If I was quoted a certain way in one paper, the other paper would take a different tack. I didn't see as much of that in Washington, DC. There were a couple of reporters who I think didn't report fairly about me, but that was the exception. They were a lot more professional in the sense of not trying to trick you. But again, I was more experienced and better prepared.

I tried to have informal lunches with certain reporters. I tried to develop a relationship, but they were always very careful not to allow themselves to develop too personal a relationship with me. But we wanted them to see who I was as a human being. Some reporters had preconceived notions of who I was, although they had no idea of my background, and who I was as a human being, my values, or how I thought.

Dukakis—Were you seeking out the national media? Would you do national interviews as secretary?

Peña—Yes. There were two things that would occur. First there was the president's message. For example, the president was saying, "We want to talk about HOPE, the welfare-to-work effort." He asked all the departments to find examples where people were hired at the local level and moved from welfare assistance to jobs. We would report throughout the country about what the Department of Transportation was doing with respect to welfare-to-work. If there was a presidential initiative dealing with safety or the environment, we tried to act consistently with that message so that the entire administration was speaking with one voice on that issue.

The other type of messaging was with my own department and dealing with my own issues. If a plane crashed, I had to go out and deal with that to make sure the public knew that the secretary of transportation was very focused on safety and that he was going to bring improved safety. One time, we brought in the airline CEOs for a three-day meeting on safety. That had never happened before in Washington. We had had a number of plane crashes that were very challenging.

I had a media strategy to deal with my own issues. If we were going to make a very large grant to a local transit agency, we wanted to make sure we got full credit for that—"The role of the federal government . . . . The Clinton administration . . . ." The other extreme involved bad news. When we had problems like we did in the flooding of a tunnel in LA, we had to go out and take care of that issue. We had a terrible train accident in Washington, DC; I had to immediately return to DC from a trip and address that crash. When there were the earthquakes in California, I had to immediately alter my schedule and fly there to work with the governor and the mayor to restore those highways in record time. To this day people still talk about our rapid response.

Dukakis—I understand that your years as mayor were not easy. But, over time, were those relationships with the media ones you enjoyed?

Peña—I don't think "enjoy" is the right word. It was part of the job. In a perfect world, would you rather just do your job and not have to report to the media? Sure. It would make things a lot easier. I saw some cabinet members who did not have the media preparation that I had, and they struggled.

Dukakis—Let me turn to the issue of integrity. What about your personal integrity and how you set high standards of integrity for the people that work for you? Did you have situations either from when you were mayor or at the national level where somebody violated the public trust? Let's start with personal integrity and setting high standards with people.

Peña—I think your personal integrity comes from your family and upbringing. My parents raised six children, and they taught us to be honest, to be proud of our family history and background, and to be a good person. All my personal values came from my family—bottom line. I didn't have to learn about truthfulness or working hard or believing in myself; that all came from my family. I've always carried those values. I've always just believed that you should be a person of integrity at whatever you do.

And I've always believed that anybody who runs for public office should hold themselves up to a higher level of integrity than people who are not in public office. That's my own personal judgment and value system. If you're not willing to do that, then you should not be in public office. Period. That's the way I always conducted myself. So I say, without a doubt, there has never been any issue in my life as a public servant that has challenged my integrity.

Dukakis—Were there situations where you had to deal with someone who demonstrated a significant lapse in integrity?

Peña—Yes. In my city administration I had a very controversial experience with one of my department heads. He was very popular with the public, but, unfortunately, we learned that he was having an extramarital relationship with a woman under his supervision. This was inappropriate, so I terminated him. I was criticized by a lot of people who genuinely admired him.

In another case, questions were raised about a cabinet member's use of city funds. I fired that person also. This was very disappointing. In Washington, I had to terminate someone I admired due to sexual harassment. Again, it was a very difficult decision.

Dukakis—As mayor, what did you do with your staff on this issue?

Peña—The first step was to let people see who I was. If I didn't conduct myself with integrity, why should anybody else? If I maintained high, personal standards, then people would say, "Oh, I couldn't do that, the mayor would kill me."

Secondly, if a personnel issue would come up, I'd gather with cabinet members and subcabinet members and discuss the matters frankly. We wouldn't talk about a particular person, but I would make it clear that when particular inappropriate personnel matters arose, this is what I would expect. We'd have that kind of conversation or I might send a memo outlining my views.

Dukakis—We've used all our time. Thanks for your insights and comments from your experiences as a leader-manager in Denver and Washington. We appreciate your time and cooperation.

Mary E. Peters
U.S. Secretary of Transportation
Interviewed by Michael Dukakis and John Portz
November 9, 2008
Washington, DC

Dukakis—Thank you for agreeing to share your thoughts on this important topic of public leadership and management. For background, tell us about your early years in the transportation field.

Peters—I started twenty-five years ago in the Arizona Department of Transportation as an office secretary. That was in May 1984.

However, I arrived in that job in a very roundabout way. I attended school in the Phoenix area and had a job at a nearby Air Force base, the 45th Transportation Squadron. I started there right out of high school. This was in 1966. Vietnam was building up. I met a young Marine who was then stationed near San Diego. He was being transferred to Camp Lejeune in North Carolina. We decided to get married before he shipped out. So the summer after I graduated from high school we got married, much to my poor father's distress. I was all of seventeen years old. He went to Camp Lejeune and said I should come out there to live with him. So my sister and I jumped in the car and drove across the country. It was quite an adventure for two teenagers. I was there for about a year and a half; we returned to Arizona for a short time before we moved to Indiana, my husband's home state.

In Indiana, I worked in a variety of areas. I worked in a packinghouse, I worked in a meat-treatment plant, and I ran a day-care center in my home. It was quite a variety of things, depending on where we were. It was the early 1980s, which was a tough time economically in many industries.

In the meatpacking industry we were paid well and had good benefits, but the company I was with couldn't compete with Hormel and other nonunion meatpackers. They sought concessions in the union contract. By that time, I figured out that the way to get out of the shop floor and cutting hogs—and myself—was to become part of the union negotiating team. I'd be off the floor for at least part of the time. That attracted me to being a part of the union, but I also found that I liked the negotiation aspect of it, including the give-and-take. I did that for about a year.

I was arguing to give the company some of the concessions it sought. I said, "This is real. Other companies are hurting. They're telling us that they can't stay in business." But the union leaders would have none of that. The union would not give any concessions, and the company filed Chapter 11 bankruptcy. It was one of the first companies to use a Chapter 11 filing successfully to negate a union contract. We went on strike, and I spent the summer on the strike line, which was pretty horrible. We drew just forty dollars in strike pay. It was 1982–83; it was not a lot of money. Together, my husband and I drew one forty-dollar check, even though we had both worked in the union and had both paid union dues. That wasn't fair. The union never had a problem taking my union dues along with his, yet we initially received only one check during the strike.

Dukakis—How many people were affected by that strike?

Peters—Over 1,200, and this is in a town of 19,000. It was the biggest story in town. Houses were foreclosed. It was a bad, bad time. The company closed down and then called us back. However, they restarted the plant at about half the rate they paid before. It was not a good relationship between management and the people on the floor. Things just weren't good.

Concurrent with that, our folks were getting on in age. My dad had passed away, and my mother in Southern California was getting older. Terry's folks had retired to Arizona, so we decided to make a clean break and go back. We packed up and moved back to Arizona, where I had deep roots. I was the fourth generation to live in Arizona.

That's when I started at Arizona DOT as a secretary. I was typing, filing, preparing contracts, etc. I was a secretary in an office that gave contracts for architects and engineers. The lady who hired me had been very intrigued by my background negotiating contracts for the union.

Also, we talked about an upcoming ballot question in Maricopa County involving a half-cent sales tax to fund the regional freeway system. It had been on-again-off-again for years. There was a vacant strip of land, called the Moreland Corridor, where this freeway would go. The state had actually bought property where they were going to build it, but then it was stopped. There was hope that they could continue with it at this time. As luck would have it, the ballot issue did pass.

I competed for and was hired as an administrative assistant to help write the contracts for this project. With passage of the ballot question, the workload in the office quadrupled. We went from twenty-five contracts a year to a hundred contracts a year. We had to get moving quickly. We did professional services contracts with architects and engineers. Unlike a low-bid process, these were negotiated.

I had several opportunities for promotion in fairly quick succession during that period of time. My father, who was a tremendous influence in my life, had told me that life is like a merry-go-round. Every time you go around you better grab a ring because you never know when the gold ring is going to get there. With a combination of being prepared and opportunities, I was able to grab a couple of gold rings as I went around. This culminated in early 1992 when I became manager of the office after the lady who hired me retired.

This was heyday time at Arizona DOT. People had wanted to build a system for a long time, and now we finally had the wherewithal to do it. But something else happened. What had been proposed to the voters was new in Arizona. It was a no-frills system with interchanges only every two miles and no landscaping or lighting. It was a basic system. That's what had been offered to the voters and that's what they were paying for with this sales tax. The books balanced at that point in time. However, as we began to build the system, the public didn't want a no-frills project. Instead, they wanted depressed sections [areas where excavation allows the highway to remain level]; they wanted more interchanges; they absolutely wanted lighting and landscaping and things like that.

The agency made a big mistake during that period of time. They began to say, "Yes, we'll add that. Yes, we'll do this." That was all a part of the NEPA (National Environmental Protection Act) process in getting the project approved. But no one said that you're paying X, but this is now going to cost in excess of that. This came to a head in the early 1990s, about the same time that I became the manager of the contracts office.

At this time we had a new director in the department who said, "We have to account to the public for what we've collected, what we've spent, and why we don't have enough money to make this system as we promised them when they voted this up in 1985." I was asked to be part of the team that reviewed this. As a result, I had an opportunity to work with the director. This was quite an opportunity; I was down so low in the organization when I started that you couldn't strike matches there. I worked with the director and reported to him and the transportation board. We found that there had been no balancing. We were spending more money, but we were not collecting more money. In addition, there was a recession in the late '80s, which resulted in even fewer dollars coming in through this sales tax–based system.

It was time to tell the truth. We had to say, "We're not going to be able to build all of this. We're only going to be able to build this much, and here's why." We laid it all out. This was a very acrimonious time. But nonetheless, it was an important truth-telling time. I had the opportunity to be a part of that.

Something else was going on as well. Chuck Cowan, the then director, wanted to explore bringing in private sector money to build roads that would then use tolls to pay back the costs. He wanted to try that. But to do that, we needed a law. A law was passed that authorized this. It wasn't a very good law, but nonetheless, it was probably all that could be passed at that point in time.

To come up with a plan for this, the director turned to the three contracting officers in the agency—me, from professional services contracting; someone who did the usual procurement contracting, like pens and pencils; and another officer who did the low-bid construction contracts. He asked the three of us to come up with a plan.

Dukakis—You worked out of his cabinet?

Peters—We were certainly close to him and a few other people. There was a team consisting of the agency's chief auditor, myself, and a few others, who worked very closely with him. He was making huge and important changes at that time.

For the toll road, he said, "Let's try this." He wanted an RFP (request for proposal) written to try it. My other two colleagues wanted nothing to do with a toll road, so I developed the RFP. I sat in a motor home adjacent to our house over a couple of weekends working on this. The kids were so noisy I couldn't get it done in the house. It wasn't perfect, but the legal staff helped to put it together. After we sent it out, we received some very good proposals. I was pleased that we received such quality proposals.

But there was just too much public opposition. Public acceptance simply wasn't there. It taught me an important lesson—you have to build consensus. If you're going to do things like this, you just can't go out and drop an RFP on the street. In retrospect, it was very naive that we did that. We should have done a lot of consensus-building and maybe we would have been more successful.

Dukakis—Tell us about how you developed your management skills. In the meatpacking plant you were a union steward, and now you're telling us about your role as the manager of the contracts office at the Arizona DOT. Tell us about your relationship with your staff.

Peters—When I was manager of the contracts office, which had about twenty-five people reporting to me, I reported to a manager who was a very good mentor. His name was Vern Doyle. He worked me as hard as I've ever been worked in my life, but he taught me a lot, also. He was the one who said,

"You can do this RFP; you can do it." So I had someone like that who was nurturing me. Also, because I had come up through the ranks, I knew how people were treated and how to treat people if you wanted the best results. I was developing my leadership abilities.

Dukakis—How do you get the best out of people?

Peters—You hire good, qualified people; you put them into positions of responsibility and let them do their job. But the most important thing you have to do is to give them a sense of direction. Where are we going? What is it we need to accomplish at the end of the day? They need to have a sense of where we're going and why. For example, when we had a new hire in the contracts office, I'd check a car out of the motor pool, and we would drive around and look at DOT projects. I'd say, "This is what you're doing. You're delivering transportation projects for the people of Arizona. You're not just negotiating a contract or monitoring a contract or writing an RFP, you're delivering a transportation system." After that, we'd do the typical orientation and those kinds of things. That was something that I learned; you have to help your staff see what they're doing.

Dukakis—Where did you learn that?

Peters—That comes from a combination of working with people and what I learned in classes. Even during the time we lived in Indiana, I took a few courses at Indiana University in Kokomo. It was a forty-mile drive, and the winter weather wasn't always conducive, but I still attended some courses, primarily business courses.

When we came back to Arizona, I started taking courses when our youngest went to first grade. As I mentioned earlier, I married right after I finished high school; I hadn't gone straight to college. I took one or two courses at night school to work towards finishing my degree. I started at a community college, but ultimately I finished up at the University of Phoenix. I am a fan of their learning style. It would have been easier to go to school when I was younger, but I didn't do it that way. The University of Phoenix was a school for working adults. What we learned could be applied to the work that we were doing. I found that fascinating. I did a thesis, for example, on privatization of government services at a time when we were trying to do that at my job. I was able to take what I was learning and apply it. The same is true of management courses. My degree is in organizational management, so I took a number of courses in that area.

So it's a combination of mentors, seeing what works and what doesn't work, fast learning, and my own personal observations.

Dukakis—And the academic work helped?

Peters—It did help. It provided some important tools. For example, I'm sure we've all been exposed to a situation when employee A comes to you and says, "This is what happened," and then employee Y comes to you and says, "No, this happened." Both are people you trust and want to believe. How do you get beyond that disagreement? My tool is to put them in a room together and say, "Let's talk about this. It's not about beating anybody up. Let's just talk about what happened and get it resolved. It's not going to get better unless we resolve this."

Tools like that would help. Some of that came out of the classroom. Book learning helped, but the fact that I could take it and almost immediately apply it was very important. I could say, "This works, and that doesn't." The real-world experience was so important.

Portz—If I can take us back to one of the key questions in our study, "Are you a manager or are you a leader?" where do you place yourself? Do you see a difference between the two?

Peters—I think you have to have some qualities of both, especially in the public sector. You have to have both attributes. But I think there is a difference. Right now, as the secretary of this organization, I am in a CEO position. My job is to be about 80 percent strategic and only about 20 percent tactical. I want to be charting the course of where we're going. What do we want to accomplish? What do we need to get us where we want to go? I need to stay about 80 percent strategic.

My chief operating officer, who is the organizational deputy, needs to be about 80 percent tactical and 20 percent strategic. You don't want to keep managers out of setting organizational strategy, but you want them to be the ones who are putting the plans in place to accomplish the objectives that you've set out. Having those objectives is very important. As with new contract officers and driving around to see projects, they need to see what we're going to do. People have to understand where they're going and why.

Dukakis—Having that number two person is important?

Peters—I think it is. Otherwise, in a heartbeat, I can get sucked into the day-to-day operations of this organization. It will suck up every minute of the day and night and every bit of energy I have. I have to be able to say, "This has to be done," and then have the right combination of people who can do it. If I do it instead, I will never be able to focus on the strategic direction.

MARY E. PETERS

In Arizona I used to teach a leadership course. I thought it was important for us as leaders to teach others. I used to do this exercise—"Everybody shut your eyes. Put your pointer finger up in the air, and point in the direction that you believe is true north." When everybody opens their eyes, they see that people are not pointing in the same direction. The lesson—"Where are we going? Why?" Without that direction, people will do what they believe is right, and with all sincerity they will work their tails off. But they may be going in the wrong direction. It's been said, if you're chopping down trees in a forest, and doing it extremely well and very efficiently, it may look like you're accomplishing something, but it's not helpful if you're in the wrong forest. You need to be in the right forest in the first place.

The leader defines where the forest is. The leader defines true north. The leader defines where the organization is going. That's the role of the CEO. That's leadership. The manager makes sure that those trees are being chopped down efficiently and effectively. Focusing on the right goals is the role of the CEO. Working efficiently to accomplish those goals is the role of the COO. That's management.

It's a little harder if you're in an organization where you can't have two individuals. But I think you always have capable people around you, and you get things done through people. There's a formal organizational structure, and there's the informal organizational structure. If the formal structure doesn't let you accomplish what you need to do, then you use the informal structure. You bring up people who are good lieutenants and put them in positions where they can get things done. Get the heck out of their way and remove obstacles, once they understand the direction.

And this is where I want to talk a little about public sector managers. They're a little bit different than private sector managers. Prior to the Arizona DOT, I was in meatpacking and other assorted areas, and then I worked for about a year in the private sector between public sector jobs. My most recent private sector job was in an employee-owned firm with about 5,000 employees nationwide. We got together and talked about where the company was going. Everybody had input, but at the end of the day, the CEO said, "This is what we're going to do." The input was important to everyone, but there was a very clear line between where he was as the CEO setting goals and where the rest of us, including myself as senior vice president, were in the process.

But in the public sector there are some real challenges when you work for an elected official. I've worked for two governors, and now I work for the president. When you work for an elected official, your job is defined, at least in part, by the interests of that official. If the goals of the elected official do not have a lot to do with you, it becomes difficult, especially if they're not really engaged in it. In that case, your job is to make sure the programs are

161

run well. No scandal; make sure you do your job and do it well. Don't cause problems. But also don't get in the way of the elected official. Make sure that anything you do doesn't get in the way.

If the goals in your agency are not the priority of your elected boss, then you have to be creative and try to achieve your goals without relying on the specific support of your boss. You have to know where you are in the pecking order. If you contact other officials who are important to your boss, make sure you don't make them mad. In government, there's more of this give-and-take in terms of what you do. You have to balance your objectives with those of your elected leader.

Dukakis—You've worked with elected officials at both the state and federal levels. Do you see a difference between working in the federal government compared to state government?

Peters—Most certainly. We in the federal government make state government bureaucracy look like the model of efficiency and effectiveness. Oh my, we do have a bureaucracy.

Dukakis—Why is that? There was a time, back in my legislative days, when the federal civil service was held up as a model and the states were in terrible shape. My own state was one of the three or four most corrupt states in the country when I was first elected to the legislature in the early 1960s.

Peters—Here's what I think happened. In general, government has a very hard time stopping doing things. We don't have such a hard time starting something, but we have a terrible time stopping doing something. As a result, we have laws and programs layered on top of one another over many years. It begins to strangle the organization because you lose your sense of focus of where you want to be.

Arizona has several advantages in this regard. One was that we have had sunset laws for a long time. Every two to five years programs will sunset. To keep them going, you have to go to the legislature. To a point, this helped us get rid of some programs. It still takes a great deal of political will, but you can do it.

Dukakis—At the state level, my experience was that if you wanted to get things done, you could. The federal level seems much more turgid. Is it the size that makes the difference?

Peters—Some of it is. Also, there are many more legislators here. All these members of Congress have their programs and services that they like to see.

I do think that the federal government has grown too big. We're so federal-centric now in so many ways.

The federal DOT has about 60,000 people with a $60 billion budget. Most of the employees are in FAA; 15,000 of them are air traffic controllers. Comparatively speaking, we're not heavy personnel-wise, but we do have lots of bureaucracy. For example, the Federal Highway Administration that I ran in President Bush's first term could tell you ten ways from Sunday all the processes that you needed to go through to spend federal highway dollars. But we didn't hold you accountable for delivering specific transportation projects. It's all process instead of outcomes or performance. That's part of the problem today.

Portz—Can you give us some examples, either from the federal or state level, when you were particularly successful in moving a project forward?

Peters—Back in Arizona, when we were working on the freeway system that didn't have enough money, the ultimate fix was to reprioritize sections of the freeway. We said, "We're going to build this, we're not going to build that." [Governor] Fife [Symington] took us through a process where we took all the bells and whistles off. Just build the system. That's what we were doing, but by the time Jane [Hull] was governor, people weren't happy with it.

How do we get this done? We started in August. August in Phoenix is a horrible time. It's hot and humid; everybody wants to leave town. We started with a coalition of a few business leaders and a few legislative leaders. We said, "We've got to get this thing fixed. We have to get it on track. We have to rebuild the public's confidence."

I was state director at the time. We started building a coalition through the summer. We developed a plan through the fall, and then wrote the legislation in November and December.

Dukakis—Who was part of the coalition?

Peters—The coalition included a number of people from the state legislature. We included chairs of the Transportation Committee, Finance Committee, Ways and Means in the house and the leadership, including the president of the senate and speaker of the house. We had key staffers with us as well. And a number of business leaders were part of the coalition.

We developed the plans going into the fall, wrote the legislation in November, dropped it in the legislative hopper in December, released it in January, and in May it was law. That would never happen in this town [Washington, DC]. That would never happen.

Dukakis—Did the governor play a major role?

Peters—To a degree, but I was her lead negotiator. She didn't get in front too much. She supported it, but she wasn't going to spend her political capital on it because she had her education bill. But she let us do it. She knew what we were doing, and some of her folks were involved.

It was a successful coalition. We met weekly from the summer into the legislative session. Part of the success was due to timing, but part of it was experience. Remember the toll road RFP proposal I told you about—how it failed? It taught me a very valuable lesson about building a coalition of support. If we developed this plan—no matter how good it would be—in the back halls of the agency and dropped it on people, everybody would find something wrong with it.

Instead, building a coalition is what made it effective. How do you build a coalition? To start, you communicate. Make sure we all want the same thing, because too often people don't want the same thing. You have to coordinate with some people, make sure they're on board with it. You have to define what's really important. We used the phrase, "what's going home for us." What, at the end of the day, has to be in this bill to make it work for you? If you can't get this, you're not going to support it. Sometimes we killed our own bills because things were added on that we couldn't support.

What do people need out of this? The house transportation chair at the time, for example, wanted the ton-mile tax [a tax based on a truck's weight and miles driven] to go away. Truckers hated it, and he was very beholden to the truckers. They had helped in his campaign. So that was part of the deal; we let it go that way. However, it had to be revenue-neutral. We worked with the trucking industry and some tax attorneys to make this work. He basically said, "I'm not playing unless I can get this." We found a way to make it happen.

Dukakis—Where was the press in all of this?

Peters—The press was skeptical. They had seen people get together like this before, say they were going to fix things, and it didn't happen. We didn't really get the press involved until the package went to the legislature.

We flew under their radar during the time it was being developed, and purposely so. But by the time the bill was put in the hopper in December and then introduced by the chairs in January, it was public. Then they became very curious, and here's where the coalition-building was so important. They went around with a microphone and notepad and asked people, "What do you think of this?" Because we had done the work to build the coalition, the opinion leaders that they talked to were supportive. This included the legislature. So the reporters didn't go to the chair of the Transportation Committee or ranking member and hear, "I've never heard of it; I've never been involved." That would be "dead on arrival." That didn't happen.

What came out of the process was literally a map, with dates on it, that stated what we're going to build, in which corridors, and when. We had a date the roads would be open to traffic and how much they were going to cost. We weren't able to build what everyone wanted, so this map provided the direction. And it included a matrix that identified the revenues and expenditures. The legislature required that an audit be completed twice a year. It would certify to the president of the senate, to the speaker of the house, to the governor, and to the public that the system was in balance. This transparency was really important.

This teaches you lessons about what you have to do. You have to know what you want at the end of the day. Whether it's rule-making, which takes years, or a piece of legislation, which also can take years, you're never going to get out at the end what you started with. You know that. I don't think anybody writes a piece of legislation and gets it passed in that exact form. But you have to know what you can live with and what you can't.

Dukakis—How are you doing with Congress these days? Okay?

Peters—Yes and no. We have some philosophical differences. In fact, one of the hardest things to do in the public sector, but one of the most necessary, is to say, "What we're doing is not working and we need to stop doing this and start doing that." In transportation, particularly in surface transportation, we are at that point. We need to move away from a gas tax–funded model that was put in place to build the interstate system. It is not working today; it's just not working. That is very hard. I think the private sector can play a big role in where we go in the future, but the chairman of the Transportation Committee in Congress believes that the provision of roads and bridges is inherently a governmental responsibility and that it should not be done by anyone else. So we're at philosophical odds. Do we get along? Yes. Do we talk? Yes. Absolutely, we have to. Do they surprise me sometimes? Yes.

We're at a difficult point in transportation, at both the federal and state level, when the public is skeptical of what it is getting for its money. We are spending more on transportation, but system performance is declining. A major part of the problem is the way we're spending the money. There's no relationship between spending and what we need to accomplish. Expenditures of these funds are more and more politicized. On the highway side of business at the federal level, there are forty subprograms right now. I got myself in trouble with bicyclists recently because I said the federal government should not be deciding where bike paths go. It is absurd for the federal government to be doing that. They took it to mean I was against bike paths. I am a bicyclist; I like bike paths. I just do not think the federal government has any business deciding where more bike paths are built. Don't we have better things to do in the federal government than decide on that?

We have all these subprograms, historic bridge programs, and things like that that have grown up over time, but nothing ever goes away. The moment of truth is coming. We have been spending, Congress and the administrations, $4 to $5 billion more a year than the highway fund has been taking in. The fund relies upon the gas tax, but cars are becoming more fuel-efficient. With the price of oil reaching $130 per barrel, Priuses are going to be hard to find. Greater fuel efficiency will mean less money pouring into this fund, yet projects are costing more. Nobody wants to say, "You can't have more money than you had last year." The fund will go into deficit spending by 2009, possibly sooner. [In March 2010 a $19.5 billion appropriation averted a deficit in the highway fund.]

So, game over. There's no big fat trust fund balance that you can go to now to tee up another big program. It is game over. So many people, and the chairman of the Transportation Committee among them, believe that we have one problem, which can be addressed by increasing and indexing the gas tax. They're saying, "If we increase and index the gas tax, we'll be fine." But people like me are saying, "No, no, no, don't do that. Think again what the federal role should be."

Dukakis—One last question. How do you develop and take advantage of the collective wisdom in an organization? How do you get that out of the folks who work for you?

Peters—Mentoring is one very important step. You want to grow that next generation of leaders. At the Arizona DOT, for people who reported directly to me, I required that they mentor someone else, hopefully three other people. The organization was so white, male-centric. At least one of those three needed to be a woman or minority; we were just so underrepresented in management by women and minorities. I think we have the responsibility to mentor people in the organization and to bring them along. It's a key responsibility of ours.

When I took this job, I talked to the president about three major goals—improving safety in the system, improving performance of the system, and getting to twenty-first-century solutions. Very early on, I started talking to people about these goals. With senior staff, we usually talked to people in small groups. We talked to people across the organization as well as down into the organization. We talked about the three priority areas and developed them into action plans. We wanted to make sure that everyone contributed in some way. You go down, across, and up and down, communicating with everybody in the organization.

I call it the "line of sight" issue. No matter where anyone is in the federal DOT, as big and as complex as we are, they have to have a "line of sight" between what they are doing on a day-to-day basis and what it is we're trying to accomplish as an organization. If they can't see that, they don't understand what they're working for. They need to know, "This is the endgame. This is where we're going. This is your role, your contribution to doing that."

That's how you tap into the collective wisdom. You let people know where you're going. You ask them to help define how to get there. You use their background. You involve them, and you reward them.

Jean Hoefer Toal

Chief Justice, South Carolina Supreme Court
Interviewed by Michael Dukakis and John Portz
August 28, 2007
Columbia, South Carolina

Portz—One of the questions we've asked during these interviews is whether you see differences or similarities between leadership and management. What's your sense of how those terms fit together in the work that you've done? You were in the legislature for thirteen to fourteen years and now in the court system for twenty years.

Toal—It's interesting to think of those two terms because they aren't the same in my view at all. Leadership embodies all kinds of approaches to how the public really is served and how policy is moved forward and how values are debated and cultivated in a society. Some of those leadership opportunities and functions involve a very individual or solo form of action that comes out of your own sense of what you think is important and value, and what you personally bring by way of vision, values, experience, and sorting through society's goals.

But there's a whole different dimension if your leadership involves an organizational role. No organizational leader can really be effective for the organization in promoting the logic, spirit, and values of the organization unless they've got a grasp of management.

I think it's certainly true, then, that you can't be an effective leader in any kind of organizational setting unless you also have a fair degree of management skills.

Dukakis—We've heard that you're a good manager. Where does that come from?

Toal—I'm really a very different kind of product than usually comes out of law school. Lawyers are not taught management skills, and neither are judges. Many of us have come to the role as chief justice of a state court system without any kind of training for what it takes to manage an organization. It's a lot of on-the-job training. That is true for me. I do not come from a background of lawyers. There weren't any lawyers in my family, and women certainly were not in the legal profession in any large degree when I became a lawyer.

My father was a small businessman, and he worked with his brother and sister to operate a sand-mining business. I still operate the business with two of my cousins. A lot of my own approach to management has strong roots in my involvement in managing that family business, which began at a very early age. I'm the eldest in a family of four girls and one boy, and my father saw things in me that he thought would make me a good manager. He had definite ideas that there needed to be someone in the next generation who could move this business forward; he was very right about that. The process of becoming involved in his business, first as his confidant and later as the lawyer for the business, was a real important part of my development.

Also, my first job in a law firm exposed me to some good management practices. When I finished law school, my husband, who is also a lawyer and was number one in our law school graduating class, was looking for a law clerk position. This was in 1968 when there were very few of those opportunities nationally. About the only law clerkship that was available for South Carolina graduates was with Judge Clement Haynsworth, who was the chief judge in the Fourth Circuit. Judge Haynsworth had interviewed Bill but hadn't made his mind up yet, so I was waiting before I put in my application to any law firms. The judge waited a long time, so I was one of the last members of my class to go out on the job market. It was a tough job market for women. I was number four in my class and one of the ten women actively practicing law in the state.

Nobody was hiring, but I finally went to the Haynsworth Perry Bryant Marion & Johnstone law firm in Greenville. It was the largest firm in the state, and I became the sixteenth lawyer in the firm. They had a tradition of hiring women. Judge Haynsworth's grandfather had formed that firm with a woman who did a lot of what we call transactional work. She had recently died, but there was another young woman who was a young partner in that firm. She took me under her wing. I had the opportunity to do a lot of work on securities and business issues, pension and profit-sharing plans, and estate planning. For a young kid, this was great. I became involved with many business leaders in what was really the epicenter of the business community of South Carolina. Those two experiences started me on a path with management.

Portz—As you've become a more seasoned manager, what do you see as some of the critical management skills?

Toal—A key part of management is having a vision, thought, or plan for where you want to go with the organization, no matter how small or large that organization is. And you need enough openness to be able to refine those ideas as the organization grows. Also important is forming those views in a collaborative manner, at least to some extent. You need good people skills. You've got to really enjoy accomplishing a goal with others. That's the difference between the lone-ranger-type leader and a leader who guides a whole organization. They say women are more collaborative. I don't know if that's so, but I know that I always have been. As the eldest of five with a lot of family responsibilities, you learn pretty quickly the dynamic of helping people get along well enough to accomplish something together.

Dukakis—Did your experience in the legislature add to that?

Toal—Very much so. I was quite young—thirty-two-years old—when I was elected to the legislature, and I was one of a small number of women.

There was an event that occurred that gave me the chance that I don't think a young person might have normally had in the General Assembly. The year I was elected to the legislature was the first year we elected legislators by single-member districts in the South Carolina House of Representatives. This was an issue that a number of us had worked on for a long time, and it was backed by federal litigation. Previously, we had had county delegations. In other words, for this county you would have eleven representatives and eleven votes, and so on. This system very much excluded blacks and women. It certainly did not promote diversity of any kind in the General Assembly. With new single-member districts, South Carolina suddenly elected fifty-two new members out of 124 total members. I came to the General Assembly in 1975, after the November 1974 elections, with a group of fifty-two new people.

We changed the dynamics rather dramatically. I brought the group together and formed a freshman caucus. It was the first time a phenomenon like that had ever occurred in which a caucus was comprised of just new members. My thought was to bring these people together so we could learn the rules and be effective. If we had had more political acumen, we might have been hard-nosed and taken over the whole thing in the General Assembly, which we could've very well done. It would have taken only twelve or thirteen more people on our side, and we could've taken over the speakership and all the chairmanships. However, we didn't do that. What we did was to say we're all very different, and we have a lot of diversity among us, but we are united in the desire to be effective and to have a new voice heard. We wanted a new way of doing things and not just the "good-old-boy" system.

We really did reform the system rather substantially, and I'm proud of my leadership role in that. We learned the rules and became empowered to be very effective on the house floor. Sometimes we could figure out ways to move things forward that even surprised the older members. For example, we changed the filibuster rule, which so inhibited the free discussion of a lot of different ideas. Just by our excitement about issues, we promoted more debate on the house floor and more openness to discussion. We were great advocates of the Freedom of Information Act, new ethics legislation, and other reforms to open up government. That group had a lot to do with making government more accessible to South Carolinians.

Also, we put women and blacks, who really did not have any role in leadership, on the same footing. Many of us in that freshman caucus were not your conventional members of the General Assembly, and yet we were right in there and on equal footing with the people who came from the more conventional, white male background. It was a good thing all the way around, and I think I had a lot to do with making that happen.

Portz—Were you practicing law at the same time?

Toal—I was. I practiced law for twenty years. Being a legislator was a part-time job. If I hadn't lived in Columbia, I don't know that the Jean Toal you know now would exist from a professional standpoint. I had a very young family. My daughter was three or four years old at the time. I was a young partner in the law firm, and I was trying to run my household and be involved in church, family, and other activities of that nature. It was a very tough time to manage my own life, work in a law firm, and, at the same time, be successful in the General Assembly. Living in Columbia helped enormously. I would get up at 4:30 in the morning, go to the office to dictate my work, then come back home and get breakfast for my husband Bill and the baby. Then I would go back to work to see what had been produced out of the dictation, take those five pounds of paper to the legislature, and I'd sit with them piled up on my desk. I would review pleadings from my cases and debate issues on the house floor at the same time.

I was a litigator in the law firm as well. Sometimes I would try cases even while we were in session. In fact, when I was elected to the [state] supreme court, I was trying a case in federal court. The judge, who was the first black judge to ever be a district court judge in South Carolina and one of my dearest friends and comrade-in-arms during the civil rights era, was horrified that I was doing that. He begged me, "Please, Jean, let's try it later." I said, "Matthew, this thing has gotten to this point, and the client really needs for me to try this case."

I would try as many cases as I could in the summer when the legislature was out of session. I would also do all the traveling I had to do for discovery during the summer. Then during the session, I would do the best I could. But I would miss some time.

Dukakis—Were the legislative sessions fairly short?

Toal—No, they were horrendous. When I first came to the legislature, the sessions started in January and often lasted into October. From that experience, we decided as a group that we would stop the filibuster rule. Many senators were on retainer for the big utility companies and the big corporations in South Carolina. They didn't care if we never got out of session. The majority of the house and senate members were lawyers, and most of them were big shots that had retainers from all the special interest groups, which was corrupting in and of itself.

This young class came in, and we managed to end the practice of these retainers for legislators. To make up for that lost income, we reduced the length of the sessions. Now they go from January to June, at the latest, and sometimes earlier than that. And they're three-day-a-week sessions. It was a challenge to keep the family and work life going and still be in the legislature.

Portz—When you describe your work in the legislature with your freshman colleagues, do you see that as exercising leadership or management?

Toal—I think it was a combination. I had a vision and ideas for what I thought we needed to do, and I got together with some of my new colleagues, and we talked. We tried to develop a plan to execute. There were a lot of things we could've done. Some of my colleagues wanted to focus on issues, arguing for a freshman caucus position on the issues. I thought that would be great if it worked, but I didn't see it happening. We were a very diverse group. In the freshman caucus there were Republicans, Democrats, small-county people, big-county people, and others. We were all over the place. We would never agree on issues. We'd end up divided and conquered by others before we even started.

We needed something we could be together on. We found it in this question: "How can this institution be run better?" We focused on the business process and the integrity concerns. We were able to get together on those issues. They transcended divisions—Republican vs. Democrat, small county vs. big county, urban vs. rural. Coming up with something that we could unite around and that would really make a difference in the institution was exciting and fun.

We were successful, and I became a leader in the General Assembly. I was the first woman to chair a standing committee in the house. Not surprisingly,

173

given where I told you I started, I chaired the Rules Committee. That committee was a gatekeeper for how bills were debated and how they made it to the house floor. The Rules Committee played a key role in deciding what the priorities would be. The chair needed to be someone who everybody trusted, who would not use the position for private advantage, and who would have enough backbone to say, "Hey, this is what we're gonna do. Now let's go." I think I fit that bill.

Dukakis—Doesn't the legislature elect state judges?

Toal—Yes. Legislative election of judges is a very old system that survives only in Virginia and South Carolina. And South Carolina stands alone among the states in having a pure legislative election system. By that I mean even in the event of a judicial vacancy, the appointment must be made by the legislature. In Virginia, when the legislature is not in session, the governor may appoint someone for the balance of the term. As you might imagine, retirements in Virginia are sometimes staged in such a way that the governor has that authority. In South Carolina, the governor's authority has always been very weak in that regard. We made some changes while I was in the legislature to strengthen the governor's power, but South Carolina is what V.O. Key [political scientist writing in the post–World War II period] would call the quintessential "legislative state."

Our very parliamentary form of government has its roots in colonial times. South Carolina had a very vibrant government and court system during proprietary and crown rule. Early in its history, the Commons House of Assembly began to be a way to interpose more local government and get away from being ruled by a distant crown that wanted to impose its own royal toadies here and have them run the court system and everything else. Commons House of Assembly was a way for colonists to begin to organize themselves and elect their own judges and set up their own institutional agenda. That concept of a strong Commons House of Assembly continued into the Revolution and then carried forward into how South Carolina developed its own approach to state government.

Dukakis—Wasn't the governor elected from the legislature at one point?

Toal—Yes, and that was true for most of the eastern states. This business of pure democracy is a very western invention. Initiative, referendum, recall, and those pure democracy approaches were not supported in the thirteen colonies. Western states developed that much more. Here, representative government was very much in vogue. South Carolina is a very strong reflection of that, with the election of judges by the legislature as a prime example.

Even as chief justice, I am not picked for this position by my colleagues or by the general public. I am picked by an election of the legislature for a ten-year term. The only way the chief justice can be removed before the term is up is through impeachment by the legislature.

Dukakis—But they could decide not to reelect you as chief?

Toal—If I weren't reelected as chief, I'd be off the court. The position in which I am currently serving is that of chief justice. However, our tradition in South Carolina has been that once you're elected, it would be unusual not to be reelected for another term. You're screened and examined by a panel or committee that is composed of legislators and laypeople. You have to go through the screening process to be nominated by this committee in order to be considered. This process has had a bumpy history at times, but at the present, it's very much on the level and results in a pretty objective scrutiny of temperament, finances, ethics, and other criteria.

And it has produced pretty good appointments. When I look at my colleagues around the country, many of them are elected. About half the states elect judges through a popular election. That is a very, very difficult system with a lot of special interest group manipulation and a lot of money involved. You don't get that with this system. You also don't get just one person of one political persuasion, such as in gubernatorial appointments, making the pick.

Dukakis—So the governor has no input?

Toal—No input whatsoever. We've had some good governors over the years, but they don't play a role in the selection of judges. One governor, John West, who may have been a contemporary of yours, appointed me as head of the first Human Affairs Commission in South Carolina. This was before I joined the legislature. I picked as its first director James Clyburn, my old friend from the civil rights days, who is now a congressman from South Carolina and has quite a big position in the current House of Representatives.

Governor West did a very courageous thing. He called every agency head in South Carolina—who were all white males—and told them a Human Affairs Commission was being created. It was going to be the referral agency for discrimination complaints, and each agency in South Carolina had to draw up an affirmative action plan to show how it was going to develop a more diverse workforce.

There was a round of insurrection over that one, but Governor West stuck to his guns. We created the Human Affairs Commission, put some business people and young folks like myself on it, and I picked James Clyburn to head it up. The rest is history. It was a wonderful time.

Governor West was involved in real change in South Carolina that began with one of his predecessors, Ernest "Fritz" Hollings, who later served in the United States Senate with great distinction for so many years. Fritz was a real innovative governor. He integrated Clemson, and he developed the first system for South Carolina technical education to attract industry here and educate a workforce. After Hollings came Donald Russell, who later served as a United States senator and on the Fourth Circuit Court of Appeals for many years. After him came Robert McNair, then West, and then James Edwards. But the modernization really began with Fritz.

Portz—When you made the transition to the supreme court in 1988, you were actually filling somebody's term. Correct?

Toal—Yes. We have mandatory retirement at age seventy-two. Our chief justice retired and the next in seniority was elected to fill his term as chief. I filled the unexpired term of that person, George Gregory, who was the first chief justice that I served under. I was an associate justice before being elected chief justice in 1999. I've been chief justice since the year 2000.

Dukakis—You described your management style in the legislature as grass-roots and collaborative. What does that mean in a courtroom where you're the judge? Are there major differences for leadership and management between the legislature and the judiciary?

Toal—Perhaps the best way to answer your question is to describe my signature initiative as chief justice—technology. I realized when I became chief justice that we were in a bad turn in our economy, as were most of the states, and we had a crushing backlog of cases. It was very unlikely that we would get new money from the state. In fact, I thought our budget might be cut. I was very unlikely to get new judges or new bricks and mortar. So how could I devise a business process that would bring more efficiency out of the system? What could I do to reengineer the current system to make it work better?

Technology became the key. I had been attending technology conventions for a number of years, where the focus was on adapting technology to the needs of the courts. I needed to figure out some way to automate, standardize, and connect the mechanics of how we manage courts, their records, their filings, and the backlog of cases. We needed a better way to move cases through the system. If I could figure that out, then I could much more efficiently move cases through the system. We needed a process instead of this big slop of cases in which assignment was often done by who was screaming the loudest. There wasn't a process for how you push cases through. There weren't deadlines or things that had to happen to get them to move through the system.

To address problems like this in general, you need two things to happen. First, you need to have a management idea about what kind of process would be a more effective way to manage your system. Second, you need some technique for making that happen. For me, that was using technology. So I had to develop a business process and an underlying methodology.

To make this happen, I brought together a broad group of people who worked out in the field in the court system. They included clerks of court, magistrate judges—who are our lowest court of lay judges—lawyers, and other court personnel. These weren't the people with the titles, but the people who were out there every day trying to run court systems, particularly in the small, rural counties. Some of the larger counties had their systems, but the small, rural counties really had very little. They needed help from someone to try to move the business forward. I got them together, and we began to talk about what was needed to make them more effective in doing their jobs.

There were about thirty people in this group. They were a fairly representative group, racially and geographically. Also, I scrounged a little bit of money to hire a consulting firm to give us some advice, to hear what we were saying, and to translate it into a way of doing business that would make sense. I did not have any knowledge in this area, so we put out a state bid and hired a firm, Bearing Point (formerly known as KPMG), to work with us. The first plan they devised for us using technology wasn't going to work. I didn't think it would be accepted. We went back to the drawing board and developed an Internet-based system to manage court records. It was a cheap way to automate, much cheaper than the enormous mainframe computers with big licenses that cost millions of dollars that we didn't have. It was pretty cheap to put this system together, and it was user-friendly. But we did need some money to make it work. How do you get the money?

Dukakis—You went to Fritz.

Toal—You're right. I went to Fritz. But first I convinced one of my best friends to join me. Joan Assey had handled education technology in one of the most successful public schools in South Carolina, and she was then doing some work for Governor Jim Hodges as his educational technology adviser. I convinced her to come with me to the court system as my director of information technology. I said, "Joan, if you'll come with me, we'll go to Fritz and see if we can persuade him to help us." We hoped for a little assistance to put on a demonstration project to see whether this would work in a small, rural state like South Carolina. Could we really make a difference, primarily on the criminal justice side, in managing the court system?

We went to see Fritz. Fritz was one of my father's dearest friends. I've known Fritz Hollings since I was a little girl. I would add that that is another dimension that has helped my management skills. My family was involved in politics, and I got involved at a young age. Well, we put together this proposal for Fritz. However, it wasn't something that Fritz followed that well. So I said to him, "What I would like you to do is identify a couple of people on your staff who are involved in this type of policy-making and let me persuade them. Who do you trust?" He gave me the names of a couple of people on his staff he really trusted, and I put together another proposal for them, and off we went.

The result is that, over time, we have received substantial support, what you call "earmarks." With what we received at the beginning, we were able to go to more conventional granting sources and some foundation sources to put together a bigger funding package. We have received a rather substantial amount of money, almost none of which has come from the state of South Carolina, and we have developed an Internet-based case management system that begins in the lower courts in South Carolina. It is about 60 percent deployed.

We have people come from all over the country to see how it works. They all tell me, "In my state, people in the small towns just don't have the training and ability and education." And I tell them, "That's crazy! My power users are people with the most modest education. Some of them never finished high school. They love it. It makes them successful."

Everybody uses the Internet now. Everybody can learn the keyboard. Many of these people are women, working in back rooms. They are in control with these kinds of tools. There are some African-American guys that never had much fun with education, but this has made them successful. They learn how to use it. They love it.

The technology initiative is how I would answer your question. The grass-roots approach means that you always try to develop something that can really make a difference in the practical, real world of trying to solve a problem. You also have to bring in people who really know this area, experts of every kind. And we've done that. From a leadership standpoint, it makes a lot of sense to involve the people who use it and who are served by it.

The broader general public now is so attentive to using the Internet as a way to organize how they communicate and organize their own information. When I first made that decision in 2000, people were just beginning to use the Internet as a tool. Now that tool has taken over our whole lives. And now it doesn't seem like a forward-thinking idea at all to get away from some of these older ways of organizing a business process and use these Internet-linked ways of doing business. I did it out of necessity.

Portz—Empowering people is a major part of your strategy.

Toal—Exactly. That is so important, in my view. I don't say it as a political statement. Public policy aside, it's a very practical way of taking folks and lifting them up, the whole engine, and moving forward. This is particularly important in a state that doesn't have much by way of resources or education. You don't necessarily have to act from a social conscience on these issues; it's a matter of economics. Design a process that can take people where they are and give them a skill that allows them to successfully perform. That's a big deal.

I would like to take that same approach to one of the next big issues that needs to be addressed, namely, the huge number of people we lock up. We are creating an enormous criminal underclass in this state. We've locked up so many people. Many of them are young, black males or people who have been in failed situations from the time they were born. It costs us an enormous amount of money to lock them up. Is this any way to do business? To be sure, there are some terrible, bad people out there, and I've written as many strong death penalty opinions for this court as I have business and estate opinions. So I'm not one who shies away from that. There are some people who are so heinous, they've forfeited their right to live in civilized society. I'm not the normal, social liberal on those issues.

We have headlines in our paper this week that there is a big investigation going on with the correctional system. Most correctional facilities are awful; they always are. But I was looking at our sister state to the north, North Carolina, and about ten years ago they went through a major change with their sentencing situation. They were able to persuade some pretty conservative, "lock-'em-up" type people that it really didn't make economic sense to proceed the way they were going. I want to persuade folks in our very conservative General Assembly to revisit this issue. We can't continue to keep going the way we are. We'll never be successful economically at attracting the kinds of folks to invest in South Carolina that we'd like to if we've got such an enormous criminal underclass. It'll just suck away all our resources.

Dukakis—Do you have a bifurcated system? Do you have county jails and a state correctional system?

Toal—We have county jails and state correctional facilities, but most of the folks who are there for any appreciable length of time are in the state system.

If you're sentenced for more than a year, you're definitely supposed to go to the state system. The county jails are primarily for people awaiting trials, who either can't make bond or aren't bondable. Frankly, our jammed-up county jails are primarily a function of the lack of good business process in managing a criminal docket.

I am in the midst of reviewing that process now. We're the only state in the country where the prosecutors control the docket. We call them solicitors in South Carolina. They are like a district attorney. They control the county docket. It has always been that way. When I became chief justice, I went to the solicitors' meeting and said, "Guys, I'm not going to take this power away from you, but I think it's unconstitutional for you to do this without authority from the judiciary. We need some sort of process for handling these cases. You have too many people awaiting trial without knowing when it will happen, and the county jails are jammed to capacity."

I brought up the issue so much that they signed a consent order with me to avoid having the legislature take the power away from them. The consent order says that by September they will have a process for what I call "differentiated case management." That means they will need to look at every case and decide how serious it is. They will need to rank the cases in complexity and put them all on deadlines. There will be a deadline for the lawyer to be appointed, for the initial exchange of Brady information, for offer of a plea, and for acceptance or rejection of a plea in a trial. Each case is on a track of case management and those deadlines have to be met or the judge will move the case forward. In that way, you've got a business process for all of your cases.

The solicitors are doing pretty well with the differentiated case management process. Their biggest problem is that they don't have the personnel to manage it. To help them, I have, again, looked to technology. I found a federal grant that helped us develop a case management software program for the solicitors that would interface with my case management system. I also found grants to buy laptops and hardware for the solicitor offices in the really poor circuits. The solicitor case management system is about 70 percent deployed now. It didn't cost the solicitors a dime to put it in or to convert all of the data into this new system. And the first year's service is paid for.

They have no excuses now. They have a system. They have the ring binders in their organization, and they have a business process. They need to sit down with their cases and get to work. Some of them are doing well. To move this along, I have a cadre of judges that I rotate into the problem areas. I can rotate my judges all over the state. They come from a geographical area, but I have the authority to rotate them about the state as they're needed. So I have a group of judges, some of whom are retired but willing to stay active, that

I put in a particular area and say, "In the next eighteen months, your assignment is to take these people and get them up on a system." And they do it. This September, for example, I'm sending three retired judges into circuits that need help.

Portz—Let me go back to the point about distinctions between the legislature and courts. Are there other key differences between the two with respect to management and leadership?

Toal—Yes, I have more administrative responsibility in my current job than I did as a member, even as a leader, of the General Assembly. The speaker of the General Assembly certainly has some institutional and management responsibilities, but basically, a legislature is much more about policy-making. The management details are fairly confined to just making the bus run a little bit better.

It is much easier to develop a management template for managing a legislature, by far, than it is to manage something as broad as a court system. With all of the various components—from court reporters, judges, and administrative personnel to law clerks, clerks of court, and solicitors—it is a complex management task.

To manage this, South Carolina has what is known as a strong chief justice. I have a lot of administrative authority. Some chief justices in other states are much weaker in authority. While they are head of their court and have some central administrative responsibility, much of the administration is in the hands of local, county, or regional governments. These chief justices are neither the boss of it or in control of it. I, on the other hand, have authority over the entire statewide judicial system, and I have the responsibility of asking for money to fund a good deal of what's done. There is some county funding for some of the projects, but my budget includes a lot of what's needed to function. The culture and expectation is to look to the chief justice for advice as to how the rest of the system should operate.

This year, I just finished advocating for a big revision in our indigent defense system to provide for a standardized, statewide public defender system. I even got the solicitors to realize that they're not going to be successful with moving cases unless we develop a public defender system.

I went to the legislature and was successful in getting them to reorganize the public defender system and to put some new money into it. It's very exciting. Many counties had public defender systems, but they needed help. There was some state funding, but there wasn't much of an integrated, business approach. Now there is, and with a good deal of additional new funding.

The legislature understands that this is really a three-legged stool—the courts, the prosecutors, and the defenders. Criminal cases are prosecuted by a solicitor, and about 90 percent of them are defended by the public defender. That system has to be adequately funded, and it has to have standards so you get qualified people involved. People who work in this system need to have a certain amount of education, experience, and continuing legal education, and there needs to be performance standards. All of that's in this legislation, I'm glad to say, and the results are going to be a much better way of moving the criminal process forward.

Legislators don't talk too much in those terms about business processes and performance measures. They talk in a more policy-oriented way about punishment and public perception. But really it's very empowering when they begin to talk about things in terms of business concepts and principles. I'm not someone who thinks business has the answer to everything or that we should run everything like a business. I know that there's a policy dimension and a political dimension to everything that public officials do. I certainly came out of a very political milieu in the General Assembly. I think that's helped me to become a better manager of this system.

I've been out of the legislature for twenty years. As of this March, I've been here at the court as long as I was in private practice. But I've had very close relationships with the members of the legislature. I scrutinize carefully what they do. I also make it my business to have professional relationships with the governor and other key members of the executive branch. We don't have to be best buddies on a social basis, but I make it a point to have contact and relationships with them and their staffs. Over time, I want them to feel that they can call me and I can call them as we move some of these important policies forward.

Dukakis—Talk a little more about that. How do you keep in touch with other elected officials? Is it primarily informal?

Toal—Yes, most of it is informal. South Carolina is not like some of the larger states that have very formal mechanisms for that type of interaction. If you were interviewing Ron George, who is the chief justice of the California court system, it would be different. He is a fabulous chief justice, and he heads the largest court system in the world, not just in the United States. He has to have some more formal mechanisms for some of the things that I can accomplish informally. That being said, I guarantee you he would echo what I say—informal contacts are critical. He has judicial councils and other very formal mechanisms, and he has organizations that are court-related, as do I, but much of what he will accomplish this year will be because he's made it his business to know [Governor] Arnold Schwarzenegger. He talks to the governor and his staff, and he sets up informal sessions on a regular basis to talk about issues and concerns.

These sessions are very important. And you don't do them just on a rote basis. You take an issue that the two of you need to talk about, and you say, "Listen, let's talk. We've got this problem. What can we do—you and I—to move it along in a better way?" You pick something that's a real, live issue that the two of you can work on and achieve success.

Beyond the governor, the same is true of the speaker of the house, the president pro tempore of the senate, the chairs of the two judiciary committees and the finance committees. I make it my business to keep in touch with all these folks. Over time, they've seen the value of keeping in touch with me. It wasn't always that way. My predecessors were, for the most part, fairly removed from the General Assembly and had a narrow view of what it meant to manage a court system. The system operated as best it could in a regional or local way.

My focus has very much been on standardization. That doesn't mean I control everything, but it means that there is a standard way of operating so that folks in some of the smaller, rural counties have the same access to a system of dispute resolution as do people in larger counties. Lawyers and others involved in the courts throughout the state should have the same access to a process that's modern and that they can use. To do that, you need a standard way of operating, whether it's for writing tickets or some other aspect of state business.

Dukakis—If you had never been in the legislature, do you think you would be as effective as a chief justice and as focused on these relationships?

Toal—I do not. Of course, given that judges are chosen by the legislature, the tradition was that many judges came from the legislature. This is changing since two things happened. First, the legislature passed a law that said you have to be out of office for a certain amount of time before you can run for a judgeship. Second, fewer lawyers are running for the legislature. Out of 124 members of the house, only about 30 are lawyers. There used to be a majority of lawyers in both chambers. As a result, many of my predecessors came from a legislative environment.

The approach to institutional management was completely different at that time. I venture to say that as you look at governmental management in your study, you'll uncover processes that are of a fairly modern vintage. In recent years, there has developed a more organized way to look at how one manages the public's business. Governmental institutions came late to those kinds of conversations.

Dukakis—How many times a year do you talk to the governor?

Toal—Probably every other week, no matter who the governor is. I don't always speak to the governor directly, but I definitely keep the lines of communication open with the staff. The governor right now is Mark Sanford, and I'm frequently in contact with members of his staff.

The communication really varies. I might get a call from a staff person saying, "Jean, we have these appointments to make. We're trying to check out these folks. Off the record, what do you think?" Or "This corrections thing is blowing up in our face. What would you do?" Or "We're trying to move forward with child support enforcement. What do you think?" It can be a lot of different things. Some are more directly related. Sometimes they call me and say, "We want to bring a lawsuit. We're really mad about this thing." And I say, "You know I can't talk to you about that. All I can say is I'll treat anything you file very respectfully and very expeditiously."

It takes time to develop these relationships with the governor and legislators. When I first became chief justice, some would not have trusted me to say "Hello." Now, they know that I keep their confidence. They know that if I have something that is really a problem that involves them, I am going to try and solve it without going public or making them look bad. You build trust that way.

Some people might do this in a different way, depending upon their own goals. I am where I want to be. I have a very deep, lifelong commitment to government service of this type. The political aspects, although they've been a fascinating part of my life, are put to the side in a way. I don't feel like I have to make points with the public in order to move to the next stage in my life. I'm not saying that's bad. Some people are trying to move up in a political world, so they can't be just a behind-the-scenes manager. Fortunately, that's not where I'm headed.

Dukakis—In your role as chief justice, do you get out to individual courts? Do you visit the rural counties, for example?

Toal—Oh, yes. I'm on the road a lot. Fortunately, South Carolina is a small state, and Columbia is very central. You can be any place in South Carolina in three hours or less. So I get in my red van and drive all over the place.

If we're about to initiate a technology program in a county, I tell people, "Let's set up a meeting with your county council—the local governing body—and let me appear publicly and advocate for it." And when we complete a program in a county, I always make another appearance before the county council. I'm there simply to praise all the people. I use a PowerPoint presentation and put all of their pictures up. I get as personal as I can, and I praise the council for its vision and tell them that they'll be nationally known for this great program. I give them a stake in the action.

I travel widely to solicitors' meetings, public defenders' meetings, clerks of court meetings, and others. The topics vary. I may lead an ethics seminar or give an update on technology or the budget.

Dukakis—What about the organized bar, are they involved?

Toal—Very much so. The organized bar was off by itself when I joined the court, but they are very involved with the court now and vice versa. The court just had a private meeting with the new officers of the bar's Executive Committee. They had a chance to talk about their vision and goals. I think we've developed a relationship that doesn't typically exist in other states. They know that we are interested in what they do.

I also give an annual talk to the legislature. As a member of the General Assembly, I sponsored the legislation to make that happen. At that time, we had a very poisonous relationship between the legislature and the court. There was a power struggle between some of the people that headed up the house and the senate and the man who was the chief justice of this court. For several years, it was a very bitter relationship that was very destructive and kept us from being able to move the state forward. Two of the people died, and in the process of trying to make the peace on these issues of power, we finally got a constitutional change that helped sort out the dynamics of who had authority to do what. To cap it off, I sponsored a piece of legislation that invited the chief justice to give a State of the Judiciary speech every year to the General Assembly.

It's very well attended by legislators. I do it with a PowerPoint presentation.

Portz—Is this common in other states?

Toal—Yes, increasingly so. Most chief justices will have a State of the Judiciary speech that they give. Some give it to their state bar association or some other state organization. About half of us now have the opportunity to address our legislature. It's something that I encourage other chief justices to do. It's very important to have this kind of public coming together.

Dukakis—How do you deal with the press? Do you have a conscious press strategy?

Toal—I have a bit of a love-hate relationship with the press. I don't have a press officer or an information officer just because I have so many other financial needs. As an aside, I represented the press when I was a lawyer. I did some First Amendment work for several of the local newspapers. I brought some of the first Freedom of Information Act suits, and I sponsored that type of legislation when I was in the General Assembly. So I've had a decent relationship with the press.

My approach has been to be accessible. If a reporter wants me, they get me. Sometimes it blows their mind, but I return their calls and talk to them on my own. Or they come to my office to see me. I respond to the press a couple of times a week. Sometimes it'll be short; sometimes it'll be long. I don't agree with everything they print, but when I disagree, I tell them. And when I go to visit one of the county councils for a technology presentation, someone from my staff contacts the local press, and they usually cover it.

Dukakis—Here's the most important question of all. Who is Costa Pleicones?

Toal—Costa is the fifth member of our court.

Dukakis—A Greek-American!

Toal—A Greek-American. He and I grew up together. In the 200-plus-year history of this court, I'm the first person from Columbia to ever serve, and he is the second. Costa and I grew up together and have known each other since we were ten years old. His family ran an open-air market, and my father used to go by there for a beer after work everyday. He and Big Mike Pleicones, Costa's father, would have a beer while Costa and I would put the peas on the shelves.

Dukakis—My last question involves mentoring. You mentioned this earlier. How much of that do you do with your judges?

Toal—I do a lot. I think mentoring is extremely important. I didn't have a strong mentoring network when I came through. There were so few women. I had my classmates who believed in me, and some people in the initial law firm I went to. But it was hard for a young woman to get started in the law business.

I think it is so important, particularly for people not in the mainstream, to be mentored. I spend a lot of time with new judges, and I get other senior and experienced judges to do the same. I have a very formal program for new judges. I have them meet with a group of senior judges, not just one, so they get different perspectives.

We've also started something called the Chief Justice's Commission on the Profession. It's a group of really bright lawyers, judges, and professors from all over the state who meet to discuss ways to improve the image of the profession, the values of the profession, etc. They come up with good ideas all the time. The most recent one is to start a mentoring program for new lawyers. We've selected about a third of this year's class that has just been sworn in to admission. They're going to have mentors drawn from among the more experienced lawyers at the bar.

The mentor will be the new lawyer's go-to guy or go-to gal for that first year. There are certain things we tell the mentors we want them to accomplish with the new lawyers. For example, we want them to develop a relationship with their mentee. This program has a lot of promise because we have so many young lawyers that get in trouble their first couple of years. Often, it's because they don't feel like they have anybody they can turn to. They are sometimes too ashamed to tell the firm that they have a problem, but they might open up with their mentor.

Another group that I think mentoring is extremely important for is women. We didn't have a South Carolina Women Lawyers Association when I first started. There weren't enough of us to form such a thing. But we have a very vibrant Women Lawyers Association now, and over time, we've developed a culture among the women of helping each other out and reaching down to those who need a little help or push to be successful.

My mantra with them is "Keep the ladder down." There's a great tendency among some trailblazers to keep their story of how they made it to themselves. Some leaders think, "If I let too many people in on this, then I won't get where I want to go." That's terrible, in my view. What you need to do is leave the ladder down and pull the next group up that ladder. I say that so often that the South Carolina Women Lawyers Association finally created a small pin with a ladder and a little South Carolina wren climbing up the ladder. They call it Toal's Ladder Pin.

We took the mentoring idea to one other venue—sports. I'm a sports nut. I love everything about sports. Baseball and basketball are my two favorites. As a result, we have a mentoring group that works with the University of South Carolina women's basketball team. It started out when I said, "Let's get together a group of gals that played varsity sports in college." I played hockey; I was the goalie on my field hockey team. We brought together this group of women who know about athletics, and we paired each one with a young lady on the basketball team. We serve as mentors for these young women, many of whom come from tough backgrounds. They just need a little boost and a better understanding of how they fit in and how they can move forward. We help them figure that out and help them gain the skills they'll need for life after basketball.

Today, we have a great group of women serving as mentors, some who never played sports. They are mentoring these girls, coming to all the games, helping with summer job opportunities, and, in general, just helping these young ladies keep things together and move forward in life.

You hit a hot button when you asked about mentoring. As you become successful, it's awfully important to let somebody else get in on whatever kind of a little aura you have that they could use. I remember the years when I didn't have any of that aura. I would look with envy at the people who had made it, and I would think, "How can I get there?" It's so easy if you have had some success in life to let somebody else share that reflected glory.

Bernard E. Trainor

Lieutenant General, U.S. Marine Corps, Retired
Interviewed by Michael Dukakis and John Portz
November 9, 2008
Potomac Falls, Virginia

Portz—One focus in our study is on the nature of leadership and management. More specifically, is there a difference between leadership and management? And where would you put yourself in this? Were you primarily a leader or a manager?

Trainor—I don't think that anybody who's going to be successful can be exclusively one or the other except in a narrow sense. You really have to be both to be effective.

In combat, you don't have to be a very good manager in the accepted sense. Leadership is what counts above all. Leadership skills involve being able to influence the action of others. A lot of it comes from intuition, experience, being very sensitive to interpersonal relations, and knowing human nature. You can be a very good leader and an absolutely terrible manager, because leadership is inspiring and getting people to do that which you want them to do even though their inclination may be just the opposite. Nobody wants to get out of a foxhole and charge through an artillery barrage, but a leader inspires his troops to do so despite the danger. A manager would probably analyze matters and stay put. That's why we have leaders in combat and not managers. Managers manage systems; they're managing things. They are far more analytical and far less intuitive. Leadership is odds-measured [calculated] intuition based upon training, mission, experience, and understanding of human nature. Leaders lead human beings.

Dukakis—Do you think that's particularly important in the military? That is, this kind of intuitive leadership?

Trainor—Leadership is paramount, management skills less so, although it is also important that a combat leader effectively manage the nonhuman resources made available to him. In noncombat environments the equation still applies, but the emphasis may be reversed.

For example, at the Kennedy School of Government at Harvard University, I ran a professional education program for senior government executives, a position that was mainly managerial. But I had a staff and senior executive students to direct. That required leadership skills for maximum efficiency. Management and leadership are interconnected. If you're going to be a good manager, you also try to be a good leader and get people to willingly work with you.

Dukakis—Tell us a little about your military service. Your combat career included Korea and Vietnam. Where were you in Korea?

Trainor—When I first arrived as a brand-new lieutenant rifle platoon leader, the Marines were fighting North Koreans in the mountains on the east coast of Korea, just above the "Punch Bowl" [a distinctive area in Korea where key battles were fought]. In the spring of 1952 we moved to the west coast to the Panmunjom area, where we faced the Chinese in terrain similar to Southern California.

Dukakis—I also served in Korea at a place called Munsan.

Trainor—Munsan-Ni was the railroad town right by the Imjin River, just behind us.

Dukakis—In Vietnam you had greater command responsibilities?

Trainor—Yes. In Vietnam, on my first tour [1965–1966], I was with an organization called SOG. It was a covert special operations unit that secretly carried the war to North Vietnam.

There were three elements to it: one was operations over Laos, one was airlifting operatives into North Vietnam, and the one that I was involved in was maritime operations. We operated out of a hidden site near Da Nang. We had PT boats and we would run operations up north into North Vietnam waters to capture prisoners, run raids, and to conduct psychological operations.

My second tour [1970–1971] was with the Marines. The first half of my tour I commanded an infantry battalion, and for the second half I commanded a reconnaissance battalion. We operated west of Da Nang.

Dukakis—In those combat tours, did you have managerial responsibilities as well as leadership challenges?

Trainor—As a battalion commander I focused on the fight and left most of the support functions to my executive officer and small staff. However, that was not true in the other jobs I had where there was a greater balance between leadership and management. This was particularly true as I became more senior. You can be a good leader and a bad manager, but I don't think that you can be a very successful manager unless you also have leadership qualities, because human beings are involved in both instances.

As a senior officer I had some big jobs that called for management skills. In the mid-1970s, as a colonel, I was responsible for recruiting and reserve affairs in the northeastern United States. This was followed by promotion to a brigadier general responsible for the Recruit Depot at Parris Island. Next, I was a two-star general at the Marine Corps Development and Education Command at Quantico, Virginia. All of these assignments were diverse with large budgets. Of course I had a substantial staff to help me in my duties.

I managed by exception [closer supervision for those needing it]. After assessing a situation, listening to a variety of views, I would issue "mission-type" orders and provide "commander's guidance" to my subordinates and then let them independently carry out their duties in accordance with my goals. I was always mindful, however, of a lesson all second lieutenants learn: "Supervise the execution of your orders, but do it without micromanaging." It was a bit like industry's admonition to managers to walk around the workshop floor. I got out of my office and simply wandered around talking to people who were doing the work at the lower echelon.

Normally speaking, in the military, if you're in combat it's almost exclusively leadership. When you're out of combat, it's a mixture of leadership and management at all levels.

The period in the 1970s when I ran the recruiting and reserve programs in the northeast was a good example of the combination of leadership and management skills. This was during the worst period right after the Vietnam War. Recruiting was difficult. The challenge was to overcome the antipathy towards the military and recruit good people in the numbers needed. I came up with a management technique called "systematic recruiting" which allowed us to do that. We solved the recruiting problem. It's really what got me my first star.

Dukakis—Tell us about that experience.

Trainor—When I took over the job in 1974, I found that the recruiters were demoralized. They were under terrible pressure to make a monthly quota of enlistees. They were kept on duty practically around the clock and on weekends. It was a waste of time and counterproductive. To make their quotas, recruiters would lie, cheat, and steal. As a result, the Marine Corps was unknowingly enlisting felons, drug users, and the physically unfit. The recruit depots were complaining about the poor quality, as were officers and NCOs in the operating forces. I said, "OK, this is crazy, it's got to stop." I took the approach of looking at each of the recruiting stations and rating them from worst to best. "Best" was an oxymoron since none of them were in good shape.

I then looked at how we distributed our resources, such as advertising and numbers of recruiters. It was a case of equal distribution of scarce resources. I changed that. Reorganizing my assets, I gave priority to the least sick of my recruiting stations. The idea was to temporarily forget about the recruiting stations at the bottom of the heap and get the most promising ones well in order of ranking, on the assumption that success would beget success down the line.

I looked at the recruiting system itself and found that there was no systematic planning. It was a haphazard affair, based more on luck than logic. I had the staff do a study on what activities it took for each recruiter to recruit a qualified enlistee. Based on usage data, we were able to come up with a rough equation for success for each recruiter. How many people does he have to talk to? How many phone calls, school visits, and home visits does he have to do to make a sale? It really was a sales problem. (As an aside, later we sent our recruiters to a Xerox sales school.) We systematized recruiting. If it took 280 contacts of all sorts to get a recruit, that became the level of activity for each prospective enlistee that was established for a recruiter. It was imperfect at first, but along with prioritization of effort, we were on the road to a quantity and quality recovery. Recruiting stations throughout the country adopted the system, and it is still being used successfully today.

Dukakis—Where did this approach come from? You had a combat background; how did you develop this approach?

Trainor—I think it was partly my Jesuit education, which taught me to define terms and issues. When I was the Marine Corps deputy to the Joint Chiefs of Staff, some issues were very complicated and politically sensitive. I would bring action officers in, and they would talk about the problems and go on and on. I said, "What's the issue?" I'd ask for a point paper, and I would get pages of nonsense. I'd say, "Point papers are no more than one page, double-spaced." And then I had a sign made up and framed for my office. It said: "Issue: What is the issue that is important? What are we trying to do? Don't tell me what we're doing; tell me what it is we want to do and then we'll figure out how to do it." To me, that was firstly a management problem.

But that was only part of it. The other part is to do the caring and feeding of the people who are going to implement your management decision. And that's where leadership comes in.

It was similar when I was running the Education Center for the Marine Corps. What is it we're trying to do here? We have limited resources. We have everybody clamoring for their particular subject as the most important thing in the world. How do we set priorities and allocate resources? What is it we should be doing? What are the critical professional education needs of the Marine Corps and how can they be met?

I was trained in that sort of Socratic approach in the Marine Corps. Intuitive judgment is very important in both leadership and in management. People that deal with futures on the market operate more on intuition than anything else, because of the experience that they have.

Dukakis—In your recruiting job, how much time did you spend with folks in the field before you came up with your plan? When you talked to the recruiters, did they have constructive suggestions on how to make it better? Or was it mostly just venting?

Trainor—You'd get some good ideas. The whole point was to go out and listen. There would be some complaining, but they would come up with ideas. If they felt that you were really listening to them, they'd tell you. For example, some recruiters would say that they were having trouble getting into a nearby high school. They asked for help. I developed what was called Marine Corps Counselors. These were former marines who played significant roles in their community. They were schoolteachers, businessmen, lawyers, or other people of some importance in the community.

In each of the recruiting areas I tried to develop a roster or group of people who we could call on to help the recruiters. Remember that at that time, we might have a sergeant who was himself a high school dropout. You wouldn't see that today, but at that time it was not unusual. If he was a high school dropout, he probably feared school. It was very difficult for this guy to go into a high school and talk to the administration and principal. He's scared to death. So I called a local marine of significance and asked, "How about going over there and introducing the recruiter to the principal?" It was good for the sergeant, and this person was doing something for the country.

I spent a lot of time in the field. After I found out where my desk was, I went out and started to visit all the recruiting stations and the substations. I would talk to the NCOs and the regional officers who oversaw them. I would go myself and talk to the recruiters, along with my senior NCO from my head-quarters. We talked to the recruiters and to their wives. The wives are living out in the economy and trying to make ends meet. They're young. They have children, and they rarely see their husbands. Both are stressed.

I would invite the recruiters and their wives to meet with me. Most wives were working, so sometimes I'd hold meetings in the evening or at breakfast in the morning. Also, we would have periodic meetings, usually once every three months, at my headquarters on Long Island. At those times my wife and I would host a reception.

I would talk to the recruiters and their wives. The wives were very, very unhappy. I was a villain. I was the guy making demands on them. They complained about never seeing their husbands and that their husbands were always unhappy. They were afraid that in some instances their spouses were turning to the bottle. There wasn't much I could do about domestic problems, but the wives were able to vent and at least learn that somebody cared for their welfare and was trying to make things better.

Last October I chanced to run into the wife of a recruiter who had served in Hartford. In the course of the conversation she told me how much she and the other wives appreciated those little get-togethers. Imagine that, thirty-some-odd years later, she still remembered. The only way you're going to find out about something about your organization is to go down to the factory floor, which is what I did.

Turning the recruiting situation around was an iterative process. The solution didn't just burst from my brain; I stepped back and said, "What's the issue?" The issue was that we were not getting good-quality recruits because the market was slim in the post-Vietnam and postdraft era. But the young people we wanted were out there. The issue was how do we locate them and get them.

Portz—How many recruiting sites did you visit?

Trainor—The area I covered was all of New England, New York, and New Jersey. I visited every recruiting station and every recruiting substation—forty to forty-five sites—during my time as the district director with the exception of one, and that was in Presque Island, Maine. It took too much time to make the trip and the recruiter was a rare bird who never missed his quota. We never saw that recruiter. He was a sergeant, and the rumor was that he was married to an Indian and lived in a tepee. But he was a guy who always had success, but he never made a single monthly quota. He made his quota of recruits after potato-picking season in Maine. When the winter weather turned snowy and cold, he would show prospects pictures of sunny South Carolina and Parris Island. That was the sort of creative recruiting I was looking for.

We put this whole process of systematic recruiting into a manual and updated it as it was refined by success. The system was adopted nationally, but while I can claim some credit, there were a lot of marines in other districts and the Marine Corps Headquarters who had input as the system matured and was tested. We desperately needed solutions to the problem of accessing quality recruits in a society in the midst of a counterculture revolution against society's conventions, rife with drugs, racial strife, and loss of respect for authority and traditional institutions. It was a tough time for all the services. We had to turn things around and it started with quality recruiting.

During the Vietnam War, recruiters didn't have to recruit because of the draft. They weren't recruiters; they were order-takers. The end of the war and the all-volunteer force changed all that. Sergeants on recruiting duty were not just marines; they were salesmen who needed sales techniques. So we turned to Xerox to help us. They had a gorgeous campus where they trained their salesmen, and we contracted with them to run a school for our recruiters. The new effort paid off, but it took the Marines about seven years to purge the bad and infuse the good. The quality of marine recruits continued to improve year by year, and the Corps was restored to its traditional quality by the middle of the 1980s.

When I made general, I was sent to the Recruiting Depot in Parris Island in 1978. The main problem there at that time was the poor quality of recruits. Again, it was the same thing: "What's the problem? What's the issue? Don't tell me how we're doing it; how can we do it better to eliminate the problem?"

Portz—From the military, you made a transition to the world of journalism. Tell us about that change and how this new field challenged your leadership and management skills.

Trainor—Yes, I retired from the military in 1985 and joined the *New York Times.* I spent five years at the *Times.* I reported to the *Times* Washington bureau chief, Bill Kovich, who told me right off that he was opposed to a nonjournalist getting the job. Having said that, he also wanted me to know that he would treat me fairly and rate me on the basis of my performance and my performance alone. He was as good as his word. Bill and I became great friends and remain so.

As a journalist, leadership techniques developed in the service came into play. Essentially, it was a case of understanding human nature within the existing milieu and making use of it. Human *nature* is the same the world over, but human *interests* vary greatly. If you're going into the third world to report on a war, you have to know how to deal with human beings not of your culture. How do you get local authorities to allow you to get to the scene of the action, and then how do you get people to tell you what you want to know? The key is to understand the other fellow's interest and adapt that interest to your own goal.

You must know how best to deal with people. When I was with the *New York Times* I covered wars and insurgencies throughout the third world—in the Philippines, down in Angola, in Namibia, Chad, El Salvador, Iraq, and Afghanistan. I did them all and then some.

In the third world, I was always viewed with suspicion. As retired military, I was immediately considered a spy by some. I carried two *New York Times* business cards to get around this. One identified me as a retired general; the other just had my name. I used one or the other as the circumstances dictated.

A calling card is very important in the third world. For example, if I wanted to interview a person of importance, I would be invariably faced by an officious *functionaire* in an anteroom, whose sole job was to prevent unknown people from meeting with his boss. Needless to say, he is not going to let me in. I would hand him a business card to present to his superior. He doesn't want to give him my card. But because he doesn't know who I am and may be someone important, he is afraid of getting in trouble if he stonewalls me. Fear and self-interest rule in his world and plays into my hands, so he delivers the card to his boss. And I get to see my man, because *nobody* turns down a *New York Times* interview. Customarily, I used the retired military card when dealing with soldiers and the plain vanilla one for politicians.

Where did I get my information when reporting on third world conflicts? Upon arrival, I would go to see our ambassador, counselor, station chief, and/or the military attaché. It was largely a courtesy call, as I never learned anything of real importance from official sources. I had to talk to other people in order to see what was going on. If there was one, I would go to the American Chamber of Commerce. Business interests were important sources of information. In national capitals, the embassies have marines assigned for internal security. Off duty they live in a "marine house" where every Friday night, historically, around the world, they host a happy hour. All the secretaries, drivers, coffee makers, and others associated with the embassy come for drinks and hors d'oeuvres. These people were a great source of information. This is really an offshoot of leadership—the ability to deal with people. Somebody who is a strict in-the-box manager probably wouldn't think of doing it.

One of my great assets dealing with foreign militaries was that I had fought in Vietnam. It was the coin of the realm. No matter where I went, people could not understand how we lost in Vietnam and wanted to talk about it. I would talk to opposing sides, government people and insurgents. When I was in Nicaragua, I talked and went out in the field with both contras and the Sandinistas. I was always welcomed, because each side wanted to hear about my experiences in Vietnam.

Another example of military leverage occurred in Iraq when I got wind that the Iranians were going to launch another offensive against Iraq down in the south, around Basra.

Dukakis—This is during the Iran-Iraq War?

Trainor—Yes, it was during the war. I was able to get to the Iraqi Second Division Headquarters at Amarah overseen by my Iraqi security forces "minder." The commanding general and staff were all very polite, but as usual were initially suspicious of me. My approach for establishing rapport with senior officers and establishing my bona fides as a soldier was to ask mundane questions that only a military man would be interested in. For example, how many extra socks do you prescribe for your soldiers? What is your program for hygiene? Before long we are talking soldier to soldier and suspicion evaporated.

In this particular instance, I was invited to stay for lunch. During the meal I remarked that I would like to see the front lines as I heard the Iraqi army engineers were masters of defense. I could see that the general was flattered and proud to have a retired American general comment favorably on the Iraqi military. The division commander told his aide to fetch a vehicle for the visit. My minder went crazy. "No, no, no, no, you can't do that," he protested. The general ignored him. We went to the front lines, and I was on the scene when the Iranians launched their ill-fated final offensive against Iraq.

When I returned to Baghdad, the Iraqis were furious. They put me in a sedan and took me out to Saddam Hussein International Airport and put me on a plane to Damascus. But I had gotten my story.

I don't believe my techniques could be called managing the news, but they certainly managed to get the news.

I don't know if we've gone far afield from your questions, but I'm trying to make a point. Whether it is leading or managing, it goes back to understanding people and developing people skills.

Portz—And those skills were important in your next career move to Harvard?

Trainor—Yes, I used all those skills when I was at Harvard. I was the director of the National Security Program at Harvard's Kennedy School. My staff was all female. When they heard that a retired marine general was going to run the program, it struck terror into their hearts. They had the vision of a square-jawed guy with knuckles dragging on the ground shouting and screaming commands. I sensed that the minute that I arrived on campus.

There were six people who were involved in the administration of the program. Theirs was a management role, but for me to be successful with the program, I had to be a leader as well as a manager. By the time I landed at Harvard, I was comfortable with both. Not only had I learned in the military to lead and manage, I had also developed political skills while on active duty dealing with people on Capitol Hill and in the other services.

At Harvard, my management experience was largely in planning, programming, budgeting, setting policy, and communicating. My active duty experience was easily transferable to the considerably smaller management responsibilities at Harvard. But I had to overcome the attitude that I just described. Happily, the women found out that I was not an ogre. We developed a close relationship that endures to this day. I also had to overcome the attitude of some on the Harvard faculty who were not kindly disposed toward the military.

Portz—In comparing the military with the Kennedy School, were there differences in terms of what kind of leadership and management were required? Or were they more similar?

Trainor—They were parallel, but clearly, you have a very hierarchical organization in the military, and that's a difference. In the military you say, "This is what I want done," and it's going to get done. You can give an order in the military and obviously nobody is going to say "no"; they'll say, "Aye, aye, sir." They're going to do it, but with a level of enthusiasm that depends upon how you present it. At the same time, you have to encourage people who disagree with you to speak up before you make a decision and frequently save you from your own folly. One of my company commanders in Vietnam was Tony Zinni. He was not shy about arguing with me. It didn't hurt him; he went on to four stars and became a theater commander.

You can be far more direct within the military about what you want done. It's still leadership, but it's a little more direct. In civilian life, when I was at the university, there was no real hierarchy. It's a somewhat chaotic organization. Persuasion and example are far more important in the academic world than when I was in the military. So in dealing with a recalcitrant professor who you want to teach a certain element in one of your programs, and he was disinclined to do it, you have to bring in far more persuasion instead of simply saying, "I want you to do this." This wasn't true with my staff. They responded well when I made a decision. But when you're dealing with people who are coequals, persuasion is very important, and you have to develop techniques that don't depend upon the stars on your shoulder.

Portz—You pointed out earlier that in combat, it's a different situation. You're trying to get soldiers to do something that many of them may not want to do.

Trainor—That's right. Once again, you can't do it from a relatively safe bunker. You have to lead from the front. Not literally, unless you are a lieutenant, but the troops in danger have to see you up front sharing their peril. There are several key points here. First, there's the issue of physical courage. If your troops think that you're sending them to their death and your ass isn't on the line, they're not going to do it. You have to be physically courageous in their eyes.

Second, you have to be confident in their eyes. You need to look like you know what the hell you are doing, even though it doesn't make sense to them.

And third, you have to be calm; they're watching. I'll give an example of this. When I was with the British commandoes on exchange duty, I was late one day for a meeting with the battalion commander. I was double-timing to where the meeting was taking place. Across the drill field, I heard a British color sergeant shout "Sir!" I stopped and he marched up to me, stomped to a stop, and saluted in typical Brit fashion—right out of central casting. I admonished him and told him that I'm late for a meeting and that he best have something important to say to me. And with this pained expression on his face, he said, "Sir, I wish the captain wouldn't run; it makes the troopies nervous."

The troops are watching you all the time. If you show signs of being nervous, unsure, or of being frightened, it goes through them very, very quickly. They have to see you with them and that you're calm regardless of whatever is happening.

Dukakis—Do you have any final thoughts?

Trainor—You can't divorce leadership from management. They are different, but they are intertwined. It's a matter of emphasis as to which takes priority, and that is dependent upon the circumstances. You can be called a manager without being a leader, but you're not going to be very successful. You can be a good leader without management skills, but you're not going anywhere either. To make your mark, you have to be both.

References

Bolman, Lee G., and Terrence E. Deal. 2006. *The Wizard and the Warrior: Leading with Passion and Power.* San Francisco: Jossey-Bass.

Boston Public Schools. 2006. *Strategic Communications: Engaging the Community in Educational Success.* Boston Public Schools Office of Communications. www.boston-publicschools.org/files/BPS%20Strategic%20Communications%202006.pdf.

Catoe, John. 2010. E-mail memo to employees of the Washington Metro, titled "My Retirement." January 14.

Center for the Business of Government. 2002. Interview with Mary Peters, Administrator, Federal Highway Administration. Full radio interview transcript. Washington, DC: Center for the Business of Government. www.businessofgovernment.org.main/interviews.

Chase, Gordon, and Elizabeth Reveal. 1983. *How to Manage in the Public Sector.* Boston: McGraw-Hill.

Cronin, Thomas E. 1993. "Managing the Dream: Leadership in the 21st Century." In *Contemporary Issues in Leadership*, 3rd ed. Edited by William Rosenbach and Robert Taylor. San Francisco: Westview Press.

Crosby, Barbara C., and John M. Bryson. 2005. *Leadership for the Common Good: Tackling Public Problems in a Shared-Power World.* 2nd ed. San Francisco: Jossey-Bass.

Duckett, Willard. 1985. "An Interview with Thomas Payzant: Striking a Balance Between Empirical Data and Intuitive Judgment." *Phi Delta Kappan* 66, no. 6 (February): 437–439.

Goodsell, Charles T. 1992. "Political Professionalism." In *Executive Leadership in the Public Service.* Edited by Robert B. Denhardt and William H. Steward. Tuscaloosa: University of Alabama Press.

Jaques, Elliot, and Stephen Clement. 1991. *Executive Leadership: A Practical Guide to Managing Complexity.* Cambridge, MA: Basil Blackwell.

Kotter, John P. 1990. *A Force for Change: How Leadership Differs from Management.* New York: Free Press.

———. 1999. *On What Leaders Really Do.* Cambridge, MA: Harvard Business Review.

Kouzes, James M., and Barry Z. Posner. 2007. *The Leadership Challenge.* 4th ed. San Francisco: Jossey-Bass.

REFERENCES

Payzant, Thomas. 2004. "Ethical Judgments in Public Service: Simplicity and Transparency." *School Administrator* 61, no. 8: 16.

Payzant, Thomas, with Christopher M. Horan. 2007. "The Boston Story: Successes and Challenges in Systemic Educational Reform." In *A Decade of Urban School Reform: Persistence and Progress in the Boston Public Schools.* Edited by S. Paul Reville. Cambridge, MA: Harvard Education Press.

Van Wart, Montgomery. 2005. *Dynamics of Leadership in Public Service: Theory and Practice.* Armonk, NY: M.E. Sharpe.

Williams, Roy G., and Terrence E. Deal. 2003. *When Opposites Dance: Balancing the Manager and Leader Within.* Palo Alto, CA: Davies-Black.

Index

About the Authors

Michael S. Dukakis is a professor of political science at Northeastern University and UCLA. A graduate of Swarthmore College and Harvard Law School, Dukakis entered politics in 1960 as a town meeting member in Brookline, Massachusetts. He served four terms in the Massachusetts House of Representatives. In 1974, he was elected to the first of three terms as governor of Massachusetts. In 1988, Dukakis was the Democratic Party's nominee for the presidency. Dukakis completed his final term as governor in 1991, and then joined the faculty at Northeastern.

John Portz is a professor of political science at Northeastern University. A graduate of the University of Wisconsin-Madison, he worked for the Wisconsin legislature before joining the faculty at Northeastern in 1988. In 2001 he served as director of the University Honors Program and since 2003 has been chair of the Department of Political Science. In his home community of Watertown, he served as an elected member of the Town Council and currently serves on the School Committee.